The Anthropology of Europe

EXPLORATIONS IN ANTHROPOLOGY
A University College London Series

Series Editors: Barbara Bender, John Gledhill and Bruce Kapferer

Joan Bestard-Camps, *What's in a Relative? Household and Family in Formentera*

Henk Driessen, *On the Spanish-Moroccan Frontier: A Study in Ritual, Power and Ethnicity*

Alfred Gell, *The Anthropology of Time: Cultural Construction of Temporal Maps and Images*

Time Ingold, David Riches and James Woodburn (eds), *Hunters and Gatherers*

Volume 1. *History, Evolution and Social Change*
Volume 2. *Property, Power and Ideology*

Bruce Kapferer, *A Celebration of Demons* (2nd edn.)

Guy Lanoue, *Brothers: The Politics of Violence among the Sekani of Northern British Columbia*

Jadran Mimica, *Intimations of Infinity: The Mythopoeia of the Iqwaye Counting System and Number*

Barry Morris, *Domesticating Resistance: The Dhan-Gadi Aborigines and the Australian State*

Thomas C. Paterson, *The Inca Empire: The Formation and Disintegration of a Pre-Capitalist State*

Max and Eleanor Rimoldi, *Hahalis and the Labour of Love: A Social Movement on Buka Island*

Pnina Werbner, *The Migration Process: Capital, Gifts and Offerings among Pakistanis in Britain*

Joel S. Kahn, *Constituting the Minangkabu: Peasants, Culture, and Modernity in Colonial Indonesia*

Gisli Pálsson, *Beyond Boundaries: Understanding, Translation and Anthropological Discourse*

Stephen Nugent, *Amazonian Caboclo Society*

Barbara Bender, *Landscape: Politics and Perspectives*

Christopher Tilley (ed.), *Interpretative Archaeology*

Ernest S. Burch, Jr. and Linda J. Ellanna, *Key Issues in Hunter-Gatherer Research*

Daniel Miller, *Modernity – An Ethnographic Approach: Dualism and Mass Consumption in Trinidad*

Robert Pool, *Dialogue and the Interpretation of Illness: Conversations in a Cameroon Village*

Cécile Barraud, Daniel de Coppet, André Iteanu and Raymond Jamous, *Of Relations and the Dead: Four Societies Viewed from the Angle of their Exchanges*

Christopher Tilley, *A Phenomenology of Landscape: Places, Paths and Monuments*

The Anthropology of Europe

Identity and Boundaries in Conflict

Edited by
Victoria A. Goddard, Josep R. Llobera and
Cris Shore

BERG
Oxford/Providence, USA

First published in 1994 by
Berg Publishers Ltd
Editorial offices:
150 Cowley Road, Oxford, OX4 1JJ, UK
221 Waterman Street, Providence, RI 02906, USA

Library of Congress Cataloging-in-Publication Data

A catalogue record for this book is available from the Library of Congress.

British Library Cataloguing in Publication Data

A catalogue record for this book is available from the British Library.

Cover Photograph: reproduced with kind permission of NERC Satellite Receiving Station, University of Dundee.

ISBN 0 85496 901 2 (cloth)
0 85496 904 7 (paper)

Printed in the United Kingdom by WBC Bookbinders, Bridgend, Mid-Glamorgan.

Contents

Acknowledgements

In various ways, the chapters in this book address key issues that have affected, and continue to shape, patterns of social organisation in contemporary European societies: kinship and gender; immigration and racism; ethnicity and nationalism; the resurgent questions of state-formation, national identity, citizenship, multinational corporations, the boundaries of Europe, and the effects of European integration on each of these areas. The present volume grew out of a conference held at Goldsmiths College, London, in June 1992 entitled 'The Anthropology of Europe: *After* 1992'. The primary aim of that conference was to debate issues of current concern for European anthropology, with particular reference to the study of those wider social, political and economic processes that are affecting change and levels of integration within and between European societies. A number of people contributed to those debates, either as participants or as discussants and commentators. We would like to thank in particular the following: Andrew Barry, Pat Caplan, Anthony Cohen, Daniele Conversi, Mary Douglas, John Hargreaves, Olivia Harris, David Lazar, Mike Levin, Carl Levy, Maryon McDonald, John Mitchell, Nici Nelson, Stephen Nugent, Akis Papataxiarchis, Nanneke Redclift, Nükhet Sirman and Sue Steadman-Jones. A particular debt of gratitute is owed to Jean York for organising the conference and for liaising with the participants at the conference. We also wish to express our gratitude to Jenny Gault, Diana Lee-Wolf, Marylin Stead, Tabitha Springhall and Elaine Webb for their help in the preparation of this manuscript during its various stages. Finally, we would like to thank the British Academy for its generous grant which enabled our overseas colleagues to attend the conference.

Notes on Contributors

Annabel Black has a PhD in social anthropology from the University of London. She did research in Malta and has published a number of articles on tourism and gender. She has taught anthropology at the universities of London, Malta and Maynooth. She is currently involved in a research project on the position of diplomatic wives in Brussels.

Jeremy Boissevain is Professor of Social Anthropology at the University of Amsterdam.

Glen Bowman obtained a D.Phil. in anthropology at the University of Oxford. He lectures in the Department of Image Studies at the University of Kent. He has carried out research in Palestine and ex-Yugoslavia. He has published extensively in the areas of ethnicity and nationalism.

Malcolm Chapman obtained a D. Phil. from Oxford University and currently teaches at the Management Centre, University of Bradford. He has published several books and articles on Scotland and Celtic identity. Among his recent work is an edited collection of essays by Edwin Ardener, *The Voice of Prophesy*.

Dolors Comas d'Argemir is Senior Lecturer in Social Anthropology at the University Rovira i Virgili (Tarragona, Spain). She has done fieldwork in the Pyrenees and in urban areas of Catalonia. She is the author of several books on kinship, work and women, including *Vides de dona* ('Women's Lives') and *Trabajo y genero* ('Work and Gender'). She is the co-editor, with J.F. Soulet, of *La familia als Pirineus* 'The Family in the Pyrenees').

Soledad Garcia obtained a Ph.D. at the University of Hull. She is Senior Lecturer in the Department of Sociology of the Universitat Central de Barcelona. She has carried out research in urban sociology and published a number of papers in this area.

Victoria A. Goddard was born in Buenos Aires, Argentina. She lectures in Social Anthropology at Goldsmiths College London.

She carried out fieldwork in Naples, Southern Italy and has published a number of articles on gender, sexuality and outwork.

Josep R. Llobera is a British anthropologist and sociologist of Catalan origin, who teaches at Goldsmiths College. He has done research in Catalonia and Barbados. He has published extensively in the areas of the history of the social sciences and nationalism. His most recent work is *The Development of Nationalism in Western Europe* (Berg Press). He is a Reader at the University of London.

Ruth Mandel received her Ph.D. in Anthropology from the University of Chicago and has carried out field work in Turkey, Germany and Greece on migrant workers and repatriation. She has published on issues of identity, ethnicity, nationalism and gender. Her current research is in Central Asia, in the former Soviet Union.

Oonagh O'Brien is completing a Ph.D. at University College London, based on fieldwork in Northern Catalonia, France. She has lectured in Anthropology at the Universitat Autonoma de Barcelona and at Hammersmith and West London College, London. She is currently working on a research project funded by the European Union on HIV and AIDS in relation to Irish migrants living in Britain and Ireland.

Joseph Ruane lectures in the Department of Sociology at the University of Cork. He has worked on nationalism in Ireland and has published on this topic.

Cris Shore lectures in the Department of Anthropology at Goldsmiths College. He has done research in Italy and Brussels (on the European Commission). He has published a number of papers on European identity and political anthropology, including a book on *Italian Communism* (published by Pluto Press). He is currently editor of the journal *Anthropology in Action*.

Gareth Stanton did fieldwork in Gibraltar in the mid-1980s at the time when the border with Spain was finally fully reopened. His work has appeared in the journals *Third Text* and *Critique of Anthropology*. He is a lecturer in the Media and Communications Department of Goldsmiths College.

Chapter 1

Introduction: The Anthropology of Europe

Victoria A. Goddard, Josep R. Llobera and Cris Shore

It would be impossible, in a short introduction, to do justice to the breadth and complexity of anthropological studies in Europe in the post-war period.[1] What follows is simply an attempt to map out the broad developments that have shaped the scope and character of anthropological work in Western Europe. For heuristic purposes only, a rough periodization is given, setting out the general context within which the main themes of this introduction are explored. In particular, we focus on the category of the 'Mediterranean' as a culture-area and the slow and erratic emergence of `Europe' as a distinctive object of anthropological investigation. As we point out, much of the controversy surrounding these issues is bound up in wider questions of method (particularly the centrality of fieldwork), and the epistemological legacy of small-community studies which anthropologists have struggled to transcend. We ask, what have been the achievements of the past four decades of anthropological forays into Europe? When addressing this question we have focused predominantly on the Anglo–Saxon tradition of anthropology. There is an element of arbitrariness in our selection; but while recognizing that there is no single approach to doing anthropology **in** Europe, we have tried to outline some of the problems associated with an anthropology **of** Europe. We have therefore concentrated on those works which we deem to be significant in defining the area of study.

1. We would like to thank Dr Jane Cowan for her helpful comments on an earlier draft of this chapter.

The Early Post-War Context: Cold War and the Modernization Paradigm

The political geography of the post-war world and the changing climate of East–West relations had profound implications for the development of the social sciences in Europe and the USA. These factors not only influenced the context within which social theory developed, but also shaped the agenda for researchers. Political considerations were particularly important. As Almond and Verba (1963) pointed out, the phenomena of Fascism and Communism in Europe had raised a number of questions regarding the character of European societies and cultures, not least the potential of their democratic institutions and values.

The devastation inflicted on European economies by the Second World War brought an urgent need for policies and funding mechanisms to fuel recovery. One response to this was the Bretton Woods Agreement of 1944. This created the International Monetary Foundation (IMF) and the International Bank for Reconstruction and Development (or World Bank), both of which were designed to guide an impoverished Europe towards economic recovery. But United States involvement in promoting European defence and development was not innocent of political interest or doctrine. The popularity of the modernization paradigm can only be understood in relation to the political profile of Europe at the time – a Europe sharply divided between East and West, 'Communism' and 'Free World'. The Cold War division of Europe was significant in itself, but in addition it fuelled policies (particularly US policies) aimed at containing or eradicating the dangers of the spread of Communism (cf. Crockatt 1987; Shore 1990). The uncertainty regarding the democratic character and stability of European institutions expressed by Almond and others favoured the expansion of anthropological studies into Europe, particularly into its vulnerable underbelly, the Southern European countries of Italy, Spain and Greece.

The problems encountered by national governments and international organizations in implementing strategies for development in line with modernization theory presented anthropologists with a challenge. They were uniquely placed to understand the cultural differences that were identified as a crucial obstacle to the smooth operation of change in the direction of a market economy. Traditional societies and peasant values were central concerns of study at this time, particularly in the United States, where anthropologists saw their work as having practical application (Redfield 1971 [1956]; Foster 1973 [1962]; Friedl 1958). The growing interest in peasant societies prompted a number of ethnographic studies, focused initially on Central and South America and on Southern Europe, but rapidly coming to include other areas, and more general discussions and a dialogue between anthropologists and other specialists.[2] It was within this context that Banfield proposed that 'amoral familism', a cognitive orientation prevalent among peasants in Lucania, Southern Italy, was a significant factor in maintaining the persistent backwardness in the region (Banfield 1958).[3] Psychological tests utilized by Banfield were also resorted to by other researchers, such as Anne Parsons (1967) in her study of the urban poor of Naples. The anthropologist was concerned not only with defining cultural institutions and values, but also with the enculturation of individuals. In some instances this was linked to the recognition of wider sets of allegiances and a wider cultural context (Benedict 1946a,b; Friedl 1959; Lowie 1954).

Although the dominant themes at this time were peasant orientations rather than national cultures (but see Lowie 1954) and 'community', meaning small, homogeneous and relatively self-contained groups, there was an increasing awareness of the links between such 'communities' and wider entities and processes. It is in recognition of these connections that, in the Mexican context, Redfield proposed the 'folk–urban continuum' and the distinction between the 'great tradition' and the 'little tradition' (Redfield 1971 [1956]). Redfield recognized the increasing globalization of relations and the growing limitations of the community-as-isolate model. Indeed, he saw anthropologists as instrumental in bringing

2. See in particular Wolf (1966a). The work of specialists in Eastern Europe became central to discussions during the late sixties and seventies, in particular the work of Chayanov.

3. Peasant society and culture were seen as a focus which broke down the distinctiveness of ethnographic areas, in that common problems were identified within peasant societies in different geographical areas. In these early years there was a particularly important cross-fertilization of ideas between Southern Europe and Latin America. Several anthropologists (e.g. Pitt-Rivers, Foster, Redfield) had worked in both areas, and the two regions were seen to converge not only in respect of the significance of peasantries in much of the areas concerned but also in terms of cultural values and traditions. This was probably understood in terms of the historical heritage of the Hispano-Lusitanian empires in the New World.

about these transformations by informing policy decisions (1971 [1956]:9).[4]

There was some convergence at this time between the work of US and British anthropologists, although in Britain, owing to its position within the post-colonial world, most anthropologists were not fired with the same enthusiasm over the applicability of their research as were their North American counterparts. Here the agenda was less clear, and the concern with 'applied anthropology' was less prominent at this point. However, the continuing (though increasingly beleaguered) influence of the structural-functionalist paradigm did result in some interesting parallels between cultural and social anthropology – particularly when the focus of study was European societies. A number of European scholars, heavily influenced by the Oxford brand of social anthropology, set about creating and defining a new area of study. In the course of their discussions, while retaining a strong interest in social structure, and particularly in kinship and marriage, these anthropologists, in liaison with researchers working in North Africa and the Middle East proposed an approach which focused primarily on cultural values.

The 1960s: The Invention of 'The Mediterranean'

In 1959 a conference was held at the European headquarters of the Wenner-Grenn Foundation. Here, a group of anthropologists first discussed the values of Mediterranean honour and shame.[5] This was followed up in 1963 with a number of conferences convened by the Social Sciences Centre in Athens and sponsored by the Greek government and subsidized by UNESCO. The discussions of these conferences revolved around the 'continuity and persistence of Mediterranean modes of thought'. Peristiany (1974 [1966]) clearly

4. There were other attempts at analysing the links between the local and the national, such as that of Barnes, trained in the British tradition of structural functionalism, who approached the study of a Norwegian fishing–agricultural village through the concept of 'social fields' (Barnes 1954; Redfield 1973: 26). He was concerned to trace the relationships between the village and the wider context, which was accomplished through the 'country-wide network'. Networks in complex societies were expected to be wider and looser than those characteristic of the isolated community, but in spite of this they offered a solution to the problem of defining a field of study in a complex social context and of tracing the links between the village and the wider framework. In fact, networks were used in various ways and in different contexts, ranging from the study of kinship and marriage in Britain (Bott 1955, 1957) to the study of stratification and of patron–client relations (Wolf 1966; Boissevain 1966; 1974).

5. The proceedings of the 1959 conference were published in Pitt-Rivers (1963).

saw these meetings as the initial steps in the formulation of a problematic that could define and orientate a Mediterranean field of investigation, based on his belief that the cultural parallels encountered within the area made for the possibility of systematic comparisons.[6]

Mediterranean values were deemed to constitute a valid object of study because, although preoccupations with reputation might be universal, in this particular instance we are dealing with a social system based on face-to-face personal relations: small-scale societies. It is the nature of the social system then that differentiates the Mediterranean from other European systems, in that 'social mobility and urbanization have completely altered our outlook' (Peristiany 1974 [1966]:12). Redfield's concerns regarding the community and the erosion of self-reliance and homogeneity by processes of change is echoed here, as change – and modernization in particular – is seen to break down face-to-face communities and their corresponding value systems.

The essays contained in Peristiany's (1974 [1966]) edited volume are enlightening because of their geographic distribution. All of course focus on honour, and the Southern shores of the Mediterranean are represented, as well as the Northern shores (though to a lesser extent than in his later collection on Mediterranean family structures). Despite numerous fieldwork studies which had been carried out throughout Europe, there is a noticeable shift of emphasis away from 'Europe' and towards 'the Mediterranean'. But the relationship with a European entity was not entirely forsaken.

Pitt-Rivers, who in many respects represents a landmark in the development of an anthropology of Europe, in particular maintained a polite and distant dialogue with systems and values which could characterize a more broadly defined European culture. The first part of his essay is intended as a general discussion of the concept of honour, and there is little attempt to discuss the North African or Middle Eastern cases (1966). Instead, Pitt-Rivers tries to discover the general structure of the notion of honour in the literature of Western Europe, stressing the continuities whilst recognizing the variations. 'Honour' is a term which is common in all the languages of Europe, and Pitt-Rivers

6. Cowan suggests that Peristiany, being an Oxford-trained Greek Cypriot, might have had a particular interest in the question of cultural continuity. Many Greek intellectuals, particularly folklorists, were concerned with this (Jane Cowan, personal communication).

makes a point of drawing numerous historical examples from Northern Europe and Spain, as well as Andalusia, which is the site of his own fieldwork and the focus of the second half of his essay. In spite of his more general treatment of honour, his discussion reinforces the view, already stated by Peristiany, of honour as a code relevant to a social system which had largely been superseded in North-Western Europe; a value-system associated largely with aristocrats, clergy and poets of former times.[7]

His Andalusian case-study is more convincing. This provides a sophisticated and penetrating analysis of the different meanings honour and shame can have within a single village, pointing out the contradictory nature of value systems in general.[8] Of particular interest are his comments regarding the community. Pitt-Rivers recognizes that 'community' is a complex and shifting fiction. The difficulty, as he sees it, is that values are effective and coercive only in the event of consensus and in a context which permits of control of information and persons. The *pueblo* is seen as a community of equals, within which the system of values operates coercively upon the individual. But the *señoritos*, young unmarried men (as well as the women) of the upper class, escape these constraints. They move and operate *within* the community, but because of their class position they are not *of* the community. They are therefore situated beyond the reach of pueblo public opinion and moral sanctions. Thus, Pitt-Rivers draws attention to another key featue of Mediterranean and European societies: their complex class structure. Pitt-Rivers suggests that the mobility of the upper classes, combined with urban life in Spain to expose individuals to cosmopolitan influences, and these influences are incompatible with the values of honour and shame. This constitutes a way of defining the area of expertise of the anthropologist: the area of study appears to correlate with the relative progress of modernization and of the 'great tradition', restricting research to smaller populations where 'traditional' values might persist.

Peristiany's volume represents a tentative step in the direction

7. The point is echoed by Blok (1981).

8. Pitt-Rivers acknowledges his debt to Caro Baroja. Caro Baroja describes himself as a social historian and ethnologist trained within a very different school from the Oxford group, with whom he nevertheless collaborated extensively in the 1950s. He wrote the introduction to the Spanish translation of Peristiany's collection on honour, and contributed an interesting historical account of the concept of honour to the same volume (J.G. Peristiany, *'El concepto del honor en la sociedad mediterranea'*. Barcelona: Editorial Labor, 1968). Another important influence was G. Brenan's *The Spanish Labyrinth*.

of outlining a none-too-clear field of enquiry. The agenda is not set out explicitly, but a number of propositions suggest themselves:

(a) The focus is on small-scale, face-to-face and relatively bounded social units: the community.

(b) Associated with the social structure of such communities are specific value systems which ultimately create and reproduce consensus and define the community.

(c) It is assumed that modernization and consequent processes of urbanization and population movement result in the breakdown of these communities and the erosion of the value systems that characterize them, which cease to be effective in the new context.

This echoes much of the debate within cultural anthropology in the United States. It also reflects marked continuities with concerns current in the anthropology taught and practised in British institutions at the time. In the Foreword to the first edition of Pitt-Rivers' book on the Andalusian town (Pitt-Rivers 1971 [1954]), Evans-Pritchard confirms Pitt-Rivers' credentials as 'in every sense a son of Oxford and an Oxford anthropologist' (Pitt-Rivers 1971 [1954]: ix). These credentials are owed him because of his personal genealogy and because of his endeavours as a student and researcher. Evans-Pritchard recognized the 'initiative' and 'courage' involved in Pitt-Rivers' decision to 'show that the methods and concepts which have been so successfully employed in studies of primitive societies could equally well be used in the study of the social life of our own civilisation'. Here the anthropologist competes with sociologist and historian. But he defines Pitt-Rivers' work as an anthropological account because it is based primarily on direct observation. 'The people he writes about are real people and not figures taken from the printed page of units in statistical tables' (Pitt-Rivers 1971 [1954]: x). What constitutes an anthropological study is, therefore, the specific object of study (a complex set of interpersonal relations and their value systems) and the method of research employed (participatory observation). Although the anthropologist is concerned with problems which are of a general nature and are relevant to what Evans-Pritchard describes as the 'larger society', the method limits the anthropological contribution to the study of relatively small-scale communities.

Further insights into the connections between the anthropological establishment and these first steps in what was seen as European ethnography are provided by Pitt-Rivers' own Preface to the second edition of his book. He recognized the difficulties encountered by his training, which was specifically focused on East Africa. Finding no lineal principle and no age-sets in Andalusia he was bereft of any guiding concept. Although recognizing that he was 'on his own', he felt he had been able to recover aspects of anthropological theory at a higher level of abstraction, notably in relation to the centrality of the principle of social solidarity. Indeed, there were important continuities with the structural-functionalist paradigm, in terms of focusing on small-scale communities, or interpersonal relations and the (eventual) achievement of consensus and solidarity. But at the same time there was a need to adapt and invent concepts and method to cope with the 'changing relationships dependent upon context' which he sees as characterizing modern complex societies. Individuals in Alcalá could choose their allegiances and their attitudes – unlike the member of a tribe. Again, the fact that the inhabitants of the *pueblo* were simultaneously members of the community and of the state presented a different configuration of relations of authority than that represented by the Nuer leopard-skin chief (ibid.: xix). This meant that, as an anthropologist, he must tackle the 'wider social structure', recognizing the political, ideological and institutional structures, and struggles, of which the village was a part.

The centrality of the 'community', derived from the structural-functionalist paradigm, caused difficulties elsewhere. Although Campbell's work on the Sarakatsani shepherds of Greece (1964) reflects a similar set of concerns and similar continuities and discontinuities in relation to the received anthropological wisdom of his day, and his choice of a transhumant pastoralist group is of course consonant with the anthropological enterprise, Campbell too had to qualify his discussion of 'community'. The Sarakatsani community was problematic: it had no structure of authority and no effective organization. Although here too the focus was on values, reputation and consensus, Campbell argued that there was little cohesion at the level of community, and instead families competed in often destructive rivalries. Community could only be defined in fact in relation to 'a social space within which values are shared and the conduct of men and women is evaluated by other Sarakatsani' (1964: 9). Prestige, reputation and honour are the main ingredients of the struggle between families. Yet while these values provided the munition for competition, they also constituted a field of what we might today call shared discourse, or, from the perspective of structural functionalism, social order. Echoes of Evans-Pritchard's analysis of the Nuer segmentary lineage system, the feud, the processes of fission and fusion, are evident here (see Herzfeld 1981).

Concern with small-scale social units, largely dictated by the requirements and limitations of the anthropological method, while at the same time having to grapple with the difficulties of defining community, is thus a dominant theme in this early literature. The focus on values appeared to provide the means for dealing with the contradictions of an ideal of community (in the minds of anthropologists and informers) and the impossibility of defining community unproblematically on the one hand, and with the ideals of consensus and order and the tensions, rivalries and shifting statuses witnessed by these anthropologists on the other. But 'values' also provided a means of locating the individual within the social system. As Pitt-Rivers stated: 'Honour provides a nexus between the ideals of a society and their reproduction in the individual through his aspiration to personify them' (1966: 22). Furthermore, the values of honour and shame facilitated the discussion, the comparison of ethnographic accounts and the definition of common interests and of a common field. However, this field was by now almost necessarily a Mediterranean and not a European one. In fact, as Peristiany noted ten years later, a new confidence had been gained in that period within the Mediterranean field, expressed in the proliferation of periodicals and publications, and of Mediterranean sections in a number of departments of anthropology.

The limitation of the field to the Mediterranean thus originated from the strategy of focusing primarily on rural communities and on the values of honour and shame. But this can only be understood when taken in conjunction with the assumptions provided by other sets of ideas derived from perspectives current in anthropology and related disciplines at the time, such as Redfield's folk–urban continuum or the theory of modernization. Much of this work on rural populations and cultures ran parallel with Pitt-Rivers' discussion of European and Andalusian social structures and values, although these models were seen as having a much wider application as well.

The shift to the Mediterranean was not supported by theoretical work aimed at clarifying either the concept of Europe or that of the Mediterranean. On the whole these were taken as unproblematical. A more rigorous approach was suggested in 1963, in a special issue of the *Anthropological Quarterly* aimed at promoting an anthropology of Europe. Arensberg saw this issue of the *Quarterly* as a first step in the direction of a comparative and generalizing study of European societies within a 'world ethnography'. This ambitious project was to take account of the contribution of each continent to 'illuminating the nature of culture in general and of man's evolution with it' (Arensberg 1963: 77). In order to understand culture in general, the models developed from studies of simple societies by anthropologists had to be extended to complex societies, including Europe, with their specific challenge of a 'coexistence of high and folk cultures' (1963: 77).

Arensberg pointed to the advantages and the difficulties involved in studying Europe. Europe demanded a broader perspective than the single-society studies which prevailed in the discipline, and required the collaboration of historical sociology and the analysis of urban and 'socially superstratified segments of culture' (ibid.: 79). Europe presented an intimidating variety of cultural and social forms, which nonetheless could be encompassed by a refined and adapted culture-area approach. In this enterprise, the principal commonality identified by Arensberg is that Europe is an Old World Culture with a subsistence culture based on the use of the plough, based on open-field villages and the cultivation and consumption of grain, meat and milk. From this same perspective he suggests significant internal divisions within Europe: the Atlantic Fringe, the European East and North, and Mediterranean Europe, defined according to the particular configurations of subsistence and society dominant in each of these areas (cf. Pitkin 1963).

At the same time, Kenny in the same volume (Kenny 1963) recognized the growing internationalization and interdependence of all economies, and recognized too the dual nature of Mediterranean Europe, which he saw as sharing structural and geographical characteristics with non-European lands surrounding the Mediterranean. Perhaps the most important characteristic of Mediterranean Europe is, for Kenny, its urban character. Ironically, many years later Kenny and Kertzer (1983) were to bemoan the paucity of urban studies in the area.

The 'Old World' framework was also used by Friedl (1962), who tackled at some length the specificities of Mediterranean and European anthropology and attempted to distinguish the subject matter in terms other than a hasty reference to 'complex societies'. The 'primitiveness' of the Incas, West Africans, Mayas and Aztecs was based on their autonomy in relation to the cultural influence of the West. In other words, they were external to the flow of European history and tradition. Eurasia had been subjected to sets of influences emanating from the same origins, in particular the diffusion of specific neolithic techniques, crops and practices. The difference between the European and the 'exotic' societies was thus a difference in cultural tradition and history.

Friedl raised a number of questions in relation to the new field of study of what she calls 'the rural populations of modern nations': the problems of defining and delimiting the unit of study when the village, in Latin America or Europe, was part of a wider system, and the problem of the representativeness of these units. There was also the question of the dangers posed to the fieldworker of what she sees as a superficial familiarity of institutions and practices. In contrast to Evans-Pritchard's concern that in this area the anthropologist was threatened by rivalry from other specialists, Friedl saw the presence of other specialists as an advantage to those studying 'old national cultures'. Thus she argued that an anthropologist could delegate many problems to other experts and concentrate on 'the observation of the behaviour of those he lives with for the purpose of discovering its regularities, its range of variation, its internal interrelationships, and its association or articulation with the culture of the nation of which the village community is a part' (1962: 05). Although Friedl is fairly unique in attempting to locate her village study within a thought-out specialist area, the result was a definition of anthropological enquiry which differed very little from that offered, in earlier decades, by Evans-Pritchard and others.

The 1970s: Expansion and Fragmentation

Changes in the discipline during the 1970s were prompted not only by the limitations and failures of the structural-functionalist paradigm and the modernization perspective, but also by developments in the wider political arena. The late sixties saw a wave of protests and unrest across Europe and the USA as students and workers demanded change in the institutions and values of Western society. At the same time, the Comecon countries also witnessed upheavals and social unrest. Events in Eastern Europe prompted many Western European Communists and their sympathizers to review their positions *vis-à-vis* the Soviet Union. Intellectually, debates and reappraisals of Leninist orthodoxy contributed to dislodge the narrow and economistic version of Marxism which had dominated both political and academic discourse. In particular, the innovations of Gramsci, Lévi-Strauss and Althusser offered new ways of understanding social systems and processes of change and transformation. Meanwhile, from Latin America and elsewhere in the Third World, the dependency perspective challenged the assumptions and conclusions of modernization theory. In its place, some governments and academics turned to a more radical (though to markedly different degrees, as explained by Kay 1989) approach to understanding poverty and uneven development. However, the impact of these new approaches on the work of anthropologists was uneven, and generally they were expressed in exploratory ways alone (but see Schneider and Schneider 1976).[9]

The Cold War division of Europe into Soviet and Nato camps was again showing signs of strain. According to Cole (1977: 356) these changes in the international climate prompted an increase in European research funding, and with government bodies and research foundations offering grants to encourage studies into allies and enemies in Europe 'an anthropology of Europe was established and "normalised" in a single intellectual generation'. This is an exaggeration, for within the discipline in general European anthropology remained a fledgling research area, ill-defined and marginal to the mainstream. Moreover, as Davis (1977) noted, the pervasive attitude among Africanist and Asianist

9. There was also some loss of impetus to the incorporation of peasant studies in Europe within a wider problematic of backwardness or underdevelopment. This may have been facilitated by the economic boom in the years after the Second World War, which brought dramatic change and prosperity to many rural areas of Europe. The optimism of these years may have prompted a widening divergence between anthropological work in Europe and elsewhere. What prevailed in European anthropology was not a radical critique from the perspective of peasant studies (as occurred in Latin America and Asia, for example), but a certain methodological and theoretical continuity with earlier perspectives.

colleagues was that fieldwork in Europe was somehow inferior, and that 'real' anthropology involved studies of remote Third World peoples.

Nonetheless, the 1970s did witness the emergence of 'Europe' as a distinctive category of anthropological investigation. In the early 1970s, however, the contours of this new sub-discipline of an anthropology of Europe were only beginning to become visible. Freeman (1973), one of the first anthropologists to attempt to outline the scope and achievements of 'studies in rural European social organisation' (a title which was itself indicative of the rural bias and general lack of urban studies in early European ethnography), highlighted the distinctive character of European anthropology in the early 1970s.[10] Among the weaknesses she identified (many of which remain relevant to this day) were the overriding emphasis on small geographical entities, particularly isolated villages and so-called 'traditional' communities, and a corresponding failure to study larger regions or nations themselves, or to employ a more comparative framework (1973: 743).[11] Although anthropologists had been aware of the significance of taking into account the wider dimension and the State as early as 1954 (with Pitt-Rivers), the only proposal to gain ground as a way of dealing with the community–state relationship remained that of network analysis first utilized by Barnes in 1954.[12] In fact the analysis of patron–client relations (Wolf 1966b) and *caciquismo* became one of the central concerns of Mediterranean anthropologists.

Boissevain's (1975) essay entitled 'Towards a social anthropology of Europe' was perhaps the first systematic attempt

10. The four analytical concerns of particular importance to European researchers that Freeman highlighted provide an accurate portrait of European anthropology in the early 1970s: (1) definition and analysis of the 'peasantry', of its internal characteristics and external relations, including analysis of the folk–urban dialectic; (2) exploration of the values of 'honour' and 'shame' and of their implications for social behaviour and social status in European communities; (3) analysis of the relationships between neighbours, or the political relations between domestic groups, the assessment of such explanatory notions as 'the image of limited good' (Foster 1965) and 'amoral familism' (Banfield 1958), and investigation of such phenomena as envy and gossip in the field of social control – in short, those issues which Foster originally considered under the rubric of 'interpersonal relations in peasant society'; (1954) and Wolf's 'interstitial, supplementary, and parallel structures' (Wolf 1966b).

11. Freeman (1973: 745) also points out that, with the exception of Banfield's notion of 'amoral familism', Pitt-Rivers' analysis of patronage (1971 [1954], 1966), and Peristiany's work on honour and shame, none of the typically 'European' areas of enquiry grew out of European field research itself. Most were germinated, instead, from studies of Latin American peasantries and tribal societies in Africa and Asia.

12. See footnote No. 3.

to define an agenda for the emerging 'anthropology of Europe'. Beginning from a swingeing attack on the weaknesses of the structural-functionalist paradigm (a theme developed more fully elsewhere, and in his later work),[13] and a critique of the rarified, small-community studies typical of most earlier work. Boissevain argued that traditional anthropological concepts such as 'equilibrium, corporation, balanced opposition, reciprocity and consensus' – which had been developed for studying relatively undifferentiated, non-Western, tribal societies – societies without states or written histories – were of limited value for dealing with the complexity of European societies. Nor was the traditional research technique of participant-observation alone any longer sufficient. As he noted: 'The high degree of centralization, the interrelation between various levels of integration, the impact of multiple long-term processes, the sweep of change that can be documented across centuries still overwhelm many anthropologists. Consequently, many have sought refuge in villages, which they proceed to treat as isolated entities. They have tribalised Europe' (Boissevain 1975: 11).

In Boissevain's view, new concepts and research methods were needed. What was required was a framework for situating local events and processes in a wider regional, national and historical context; one that would also enable the anthropologist to examine the links between different levels of organization (local, regional, national; core and periphery). In short, an anthropology of Europe needed to focus on the interrelationship between local events and macro social processes of 'state formation, national integration, industrialization, urbanization, bureaucratization, class conflict and commercialization' (Boissevain 1975: 11) – processes whose origins lie beyond the community. However, his claim (1975: 16) that 'the contributors to this volume thus provide a first attempt at developing what could be called an anthropology of national and supra-national processes' was perhaps overstated, as few of the papers actually tackled these themes in any depth. Moreover, by justifying the case for an 'anthropology of Europe' in terms of lessons to be gained for 'poorer societies' further down the road to modernization, Boissevain moved perilously close to the old modernization paradigm. As in earlier instances where

13. Cf. Boissevain 1974. However, much of Boissevain's earlier work, was itself typically functionalist in style and theoretical orientation (cf. Boissevain 1966; 1969).

anthropologists (for example Gluckman) attempted to break new ground, they were thwarted by the constraints of structural-functionalist theory and methodology. Nonetheless, the volume provided a refreshing alternative to the polarizations and reifications typical of most traditional, ahistorical ethnographic studies of European societies, and the 'village-outwards' perspective adopted by most of the contributors paved the way for further work of this nature. Moreover, Boissevain's emphasis on 'processes' and 'relationships' between levels of organization avoided the need to try and reify Europe as a particular 'culture area', a concept which was increasingly central to anglophone anthropologists working in the Mediterranean.[14]

During the 1970s anthropological interest in Europe increased dramatically. By 1973 the number of social anthropological publications on Europe was almost equal to that of the of the entire previous decade (Freeman 1973: 743). Several factors fuelled this interest in Europe. One was the increase in postgraduate students of anthropology on either side of the Atlantic, and the fact that Europe represented a relatively unexplored frontier. Another was the shortage of research funds due to the increased number of applicants and the tightening of government purse-strings to counter student unrest. In this respect, Europeanists were at an advantage. As Boissevain (1975: 11) points out, 'it generally costs less to study a neighbour than to mount an expedition to the New Guinea highlands'.

Increased anthropological interest in Europe was also prompted by changes in the world economy and shifts in global political alignments. As Cole (1977) argues, anthropologists began to find themselves no longer welcome in the newly liberated post-colonial nations as anti-colonialist sentiment and suspicion of Western development projects spread throughout the emergent states of

14. A common denominator to most of those who shaped the anthropology of the Mediterranean as a 'culture area' was the fact that they conducted their research in the northern Mediterranean countries. The key features that were posited as characteristic of 'the Mediterranean' as a unit were only typical of those parts of Southern Europe which, although sharing Graeco–Roman and Christian traditions, were under Islamic rule for a number of centuries. We are referring to the southern parts of Portugal, Spain and Italy, as well as to Malta, Cyprus and many parts of the Balkans, including Greece. This point was made with force by Boissevain and Blok (1974). Unfortunately, that text received scant attention, with the consequence that the idea of the whole Mediterranean area as a cultural unit made constant progress. What should have been a construct identified with a cluster of cultural features which had a limited but meaningful geographical application became an unmanageable contraption which not only led many anthropologists astray, but generated countless sterile controversies.

Africa and Asia. With these doors closed, Western anthropologists increasingly turned their attention, and their careers, to rural Europe and the Mediterranean, one of the few areas still open to them.

While the idea of 'tradition versus modernity' continued to imbue European ethnographic studies throughout the early 1970s, some anthropologists began to explore new models. One alternative to functionalism was the 'action' approach, pioneered by Barth (1966; 1969), Goffman (1959), and Barnes (1972), and elaborated, in European anthropology, in the work of Boissevain and Bailey and their students. Their work focused on individuals and the stratagems they employ within a given socio-political framework. 'Action theory' covered a variety of approaches, including transactionalism, network analysis, systems analysis and game theory. What united them was an emphasis on the dynamic character of interpersonal exchanges. Instead of looking at the individual as a passive and obedient slave to group norms and pressures, Boissevain stressed that 'it is important to see him as an entrepreneur who tries to manipulate norms and relationships for his own social and psychological benefit' (Boissevain 1974: 6). The notion of the self-seeking entrepreneur manipulating social networks and cultural codes in order to maximize personal gain became a key premise of the transactionalist approach. As Bailey (1971: xi) summed it up in relation to his own work on the micro-politics of gossip and reputation management: 'The politicians ... who appear in this book are all caught in the act of outmanoeuvring one another, of knifing one another in the back, of tripping one another up, and they all appear to be engrossed in winning a victory over someone.' This approach facilitated the continuing emphasis on small-scale community studies, since it allowed politics to be defined as operative at the local level alone.

While some advocates saw transactionalism simply as a supplement to functionalist analysis, others claimed it had universal application and a much deeper theoretical significance. The extreme transactionalist position as developed by Barth (1959) held that the interaction of all these self-seeking individuals gives society its dynamic, which in turn is the basis for all social processes, including social change. What we call 'society' is thus, in effect, no more than the sum of these individual transactions. This approach ignored culture-area boundaries and historical specificities, and enabled an unproblematic shift from European contexts to others. The reason for this was the underlying assumption of universal patterns of behaviour, motivation and rationality. However, as critics pointed out, Barth could just as well be discussing Norwegian fishermen as the Yusufzai Pakhtuns, since their rationality and behaviour are seen as essentially the same and, in spite of ethnographic detail in the Pakhtun study, the local historical, class and other systemic constraints are ignored (cf. Asad 1972; Ahmed 1976). In spite of numerous studies in the European context, by universalizing a specific rationality and neglecting historical specificities, transactionalists made little impact on the development of an anthropology of Europe.

Despite these criticisms, Kapferer nevertheless felt justified in claiming (1976: 2) that transactionalism marked a 'paradigm shift' in social anthropology. For European anthropologists it did provide new research foci and a framework for analyzing elements of the complexity of European societies that had been invisible to functionalist analysis – even if its micro-perspective tended to obscure the wider picture. However, that shift of focus led to the elaboration of a number of new analytical concepts, as well as to a re-evaluation of some old concerns, such as 'patron–client relations', 'micro-politics', 'brokers', 'middlemen', 'informal and non-corporate groups', 'cliques', 'factions and action-sets' and 'instrumental friendship' (cf. Banton 1966; Bailey 1971; 1973; Blok 1974; Boissevain 1966, 1968, 1974; Gellner and Waterbury 1977; Wolf 1966b).

If one response to the critique of structural-functionalism was a theoretical shift of emphasis towards individual behaviour and 'informal' codes, another was towards a semiotic approach inspired by the work of Lévi-Strauss, Leach and Douglas. Here the primary objects of investigation were the deeper structures (cognitive and symbolic) underlying surface phenomena: the idea being that cultural arrangements can be 'read' as languages, reflecting an underlying classificatory code or symbolic order. Yet while this method had great appeal within the discipline in general, it had less impact in European anthropology than elsewhere, perhaps because the structuralist method was perceived to have greater analytical power in seemingly more 'bounded' societies, without written histories or complex state structures. However, the Oxford seminars which aimed at reassessing anthropological material through the structuralist framework provided an opportunity for researchers in European societies to locate their material within a broader comparative framework and obviate the limitations of 'the Mediterranean', or for that matter Europe. At the same time they facilitated the emergence of a fairly coherent body of research, particularly in Greece, where an interesting intellectual genealogy emerged (du Boulay 1974; Hirschon 1978; Dubisch 1983; Herzfeld 1987).

Within European anthropology the structuralist approach was used with some skill in interpreting indigenous beliefs concerning honour and shame (Blok 1981), the Greek vampire (Du Boulay 1974), the 'evil eye' (Herzfeld 1981) and Gypsy pollution taboos (Okely 1977). Structuralist methods were also adapted with variable success for analysing gender relations in Europe (Hirschon 1978; Okely 1977), though more often than not these resulted in reified sets of binary oppositions purporting to reveal complex principles of gender complementarity and fundamental symbolic ordering principles such as an 'inside – outside' dualism, or ancient structures of circular reciprocity (Ott 1981). Perhaps the most enduring impact of Lévi-Straussian structuralism on the anthropology of Europe has been, unsuprisingly, in the field of kinship studies, particularly as developed in France, Spain and elsewhere in Europe (see Goddard, this volume, chapter 3).

A third development arising from the critique of functionalism was towards a more global perspective, with a theoretical emphasis on the wider political, economic and historical contexts within which local social relations are embedded. Whereas traditional anthropological monographs had relegated history to the status of a minor background detail to be glossed over in cursory introduction to 'the setting', some of the more innovative anthropological studies in the 1970s adopted a more rigorous historical perspective (cf. Blok 1974; Cutileiro 1971) – an approach that Davis (1977) argued was specifically lacking but necessary in the anthropology of the Mediterranean.

Concomitant with these developments was a more radical reappraisal of anthropology in general. The critique of anthropology's colonial heritage further undermined certainties regarding the validity of dichotomies such as traditional/modern societies, primitive/complex, static/historical. The erosion of the exotic as the object of study strengthened the claims to legitimacy by anthropologists working in Europe. The radical critique furthermore helped to shift the anthropological gaze from the norms and values operating within small-scale societies towards the wider political and economic systems and their impact on local processes (cf. Cole 1977; Schneider and Schneider 1976; White 1980).

Yet none of the alternatives to structural-functionalism that arose during the 1970s in themselves either dominated or defined the character of 'European anthropology'. What they did do, however, was to broaden the scope of European anthropology. In this way, they helped to stimulate new and more imaginative ways of analysing social systems and cultural phenomena in Europe, but also led often to theoretical disunity, fragmentation, and competition. While anthropology in Europe benefited from this plurality of approaches, the anthropology 'of' Europe, alluded to by Boissevain and his colleagues, remained a largely unchartered and undefined project, but at least now it appeared a more feasible possibility with the introduction of perspectives which were more sensitive to historical and global determinations. And yet the bulk of research was still concentrated in the Mediterranean, as testified by Davis' comprehensive volume (1977), which brought together different aspects of research in this area.

The 1980s: The Re-Emergence of Europe?

If anything, what defines the 1980s and beyond is extreme complexity. Three major political factors should be taken into account in any attempt to characterize this period; the return of radical conservatism, with its associated neoliberal economic policies; the prospect of an ever wider and deeper European Community; and the collapse of 'real socialism' in Eastern Europe, with its inevitable spillover into political and academic debates concerning models of society. Within anthropology, the period was dominated by increasing relativism, uncertainty and preoccupations with issues of method.

Those approaches most associated with 'positivism' (structural-functionalism, structuralism, scientific Marxism, cultural materialism, etc.) came under heavy attack from an uneasy alliance of approaches within postmodernism, feminism, thirdworldism (cf. Llobera 1993) which tended to privilege the subjective moment in the process of research and give primacy to deconstruction, textuality and the politics of identity. The anthropological mirror was no longer science, but specific political agendas which the discipline was criticized for neglecting. While the conservatism of the anthropological profession may have prevented a more generalized upheaval within the discipline, there is little doubt that anthropology's scientific self-image was on the wane. This growing distrust of science was illustrated most notably in the 1988 meeting of the Group for Debates in Anthropological Theory, which voted decisively against the motion that 'social anthropology is a generalising science or it is nothing'.[15] Without a major change of direction, anthropology risks being relegated to a mere subheading of cultural criticism (cf. Llobera 1993).

Towards the end of the period under consideration the prospects for an anthropology of Europe were greatly enhanced, while the idea of an anthropology of the 'Mediterranean' was clearly receding. The momentum generated by the process of European integration, particularly the incorporation of 'Mediterranean' countries such as Greece, Spain and Portugal into the European Community (EC), undoubtedly played a major role in encouraging the conceptualization of Europe as a united whole. This tendency was further heightened with the political, cultural and (hopefully) economic return to Europe of the eastern European ex-Soviet satellites. While throughout the Cold War era political discourses typically emphasized the differences separating eastern and western Europe, or northern and southern Europe, the present trend in popular representations of Europe is to focus on similarities and areas of convergence. But it is not only the present (and the future) which is at stake; the past is also being reappraised in the light of what is considered quintessentially European. There has thus been a necessary search for the roots of Europeanness in history, religion, science and culture (Shore and Black, this volume, chapter 13).

An important ASA monograph, *Anthropology at Home*, was published in 1985 (Jackson 1985). The collection is concerned mostly with Europe, both West and East. At stake is essentially the issue of whether doing research in one's own culture, a European one to boot, is methodologically different from the traditional ethnographic pursuit in alien cultures. Perhaps one of the obvious conclusions is that 'the anthropologist at home' can no longer be a jack-of-all-trades, and that collaboration with folklorists,

15. This was a meeting organized by the Group for Debates in Anthropological Theory (GDAT) held at Manchester University.

sociologists, historians, etc. is the order of the day.

In their short survey of the 'ethnology' of France, Cuisinier and Segalen (1993) find it difficult to define the specificity of this discipline. Certainly, fieldwork figures prominently in their characterization of ethnology; they seem also to reject the regional approach in favour of a 'diversity of cultural identities' (1993: 121), some regional, some cutting across regions. On the other hand, in Cuisinier's *Ethnologie de l'Europe* (1993), the approach is different. The term 'ethnology' refers to a historically informed knowledge of the European ethnies, with their cultural patrimony and political projects and the conflicts that arise from their encounters.

Segalen (1989) emphasizes the importance of what she calls a 'European ethnological dialogue' (1989: 11) of the different anthropological approaches which exist across Europe. For Augé, in this edited volume, the anthropology of Europe becomes a sort of duty, because European societies are multiethnic, and only anthropology can cut through the singularity of these different groups. There are also a number of areas in which anthropology excels: questions of meaning, the self and the other, order and disorder, the nature of the social, etc.

Despite the ascendancy of Europe as an object of anthropological investigation, the 1980s also witnessed a revival of the idea of the 'Mediterranean' as a culture area, particularly in the work of David Gilmore (1982;1987). While even Pitt-Rivers, considered one of the founding fathers of Mediterranean anthropology, acknowledged the 'Mediterranean' to be merely a 'concept of heuristic convenience, not a culture area in the sense given this phrase by American cultural anthropology' (1977: viii), Gilmore (1987) and his colleagues persevered in the attempt to revitalize the Mediterranean as a relatively distinct homogenizing construct. However, apart from sharing the increasingly polluted waters of the Mediterranean Sea, there is little substance to the invented 'Mediterranean traits'. Too many anomalies had to be accommodated within the 'Mediterranean' straitjacket for this to be considered a useful concept, particularly when it is taken to include North Africa as well as Southern Europe. In fact, comparative analyses within the 'Mediterranean' framework were few and far between, and, after the 1960s comparisons between northern and southern shores were particularly rare. In any case, the most stimulating comparisons were not generated by any methodological rigour that the Mediterranean as a construct might provide, but rather underscored the brilliant qualities of an individual researcher (cf. Davis 1977).

Gilmore's insistence on the need to combine a variety of dimensions to define the cultural unity of the Mediterranean (1982: 184) seemed to find its forte in a resurrection of the honour and shame syndrome (1987: 3). Although some of the papers included in Gilmore's edited volume challenge the 'Mediterranean' in general and the adequacy of the honour and shame distinction in particular, the author concludes that the 'poetics of manhood' (Herzfeld *dixit*) 'would be most keenly appreciated by men in Sicily, or Andalusia, or Turkey, or Tunisia, rather than in other places distant from the Middle Sea' (1987: 16). The fact that the 'male contests' he is alluding to may not be so readily recognized by men in northern Portugal, or Catalonia, or Provence, or Lombardy, is simply ignored.

A totally different agenda, far from the appealing primitivism of honour and shame, was proposed in an important introduction to a collection of papers edited by Grillo (1980). Grillo argues that 'Europe constitutes a meaningful object of social investigation' (1980: 3), but that anthropologists in Europe have tended to focus on topics which ignore the potentially structuring factors. The persisting emphasis on rural community studies or on marginal and maverick social groups has been the stock and trade of the discipline's ventures in Europe. According to Grillo, a proper anthropology of Europe would have to tackle a number of issues hitherto ignored by the current practitioners. These include, *inter alia*: state formation, nation integration, industrialization, urbanization, bureaucratisation, class conflict and commercialization (ibid.:5). Inevitably, these tasks would lead the anthropologists, *pace* Boissevain, well beyond community studies and into collaboration with other disciplines, namely history, sociology, political science, etc. The distinctiveness of anthropology could still be preserved, provided that the discipline focus on 'total social facts' (Mauss) and emphasize the interstitial spaces between micro and macro, local and national, or the whole and its parts (Grillo 1980: 7).

The habits and practices of 'Mediterraneanist' anthropologists were challenged in an article by Llobera (1986), which reiterated criticisms previously advanced by Boissevain, Crump, Grillo and others, concerning the centrality of fieldwork. Llobera argued that many of the shortcomings of the subdiscipline, namely its fundamental ahistoricity and its reluctance to engage in constructive comparisons, followed from its preoccupation with fieldwork, a research technique many anthropologists had taken to be not only entirely unproblematic, but also the *raison d'être* of the discipline.

Llobera's paper also challenged the uncertainty within the discipline concerning the 'Mediterranean' as a cultural area. While many anthropologists paid lip-service to the idea that such a construct was bankrupt, in practice they continued to operate within its boundaries. By the end of the decade anthropologists were still attacking the non-viability of `Mediterraneanist' discourse (cf. Herzfeld 1987; Pina-Cabral 1989). Yet perspectives were changing. A sign of the new times is the predominance of the word `Europe' in the anthropological discourse; it is used as a term of reference for titles of books and articles, for research projects and for departmental specializations – whereas in the past the word `Mediterranean' would have been, in one way or another, a compulsory word in similar contexts. How far this was the result of internal dynamics (conceptual criticism of the construct) or external pressures (the influence of the European Community) is difficult to determine. In all probability it was a combination of both. Even those who, like Magnarella (1993), are still trying to conceptualize the Mediterranean, discuss the interface between different zones of the Mediterranean, and refrain from involving a single, uniform cultural area. However, it would still be premature to assume that the `Mediterraneanist' discourse is defunct. It will survive in often disguised and diluted forms, if only because there are vested interests both political and academic around it.

Anthropology and the Concept of 'Europe'

Any anthropology *of* Europe, as distinct from anthropology *in* Europe, must contend, at the outset, with two sets of questions. Firstly, what exactly is this entity called 'Europe,' how should we conceptualize it, and what are the distinguishing characteristics that set it apart from other regions of the world? Secondly, and perhaps even more problematic, to what extent does the concept of Europe constitute a meaningful object of anthropological enquiry? If we cannot even agree on a shared definition of the enigmatic and elusive term Europe, the prospects of being able to study it anthropologically might appear to be somewhat limited. Furthermore, in view of the differences and divergences which exist within European societies at all levels, does it make any sense to speak of Europe as a discrete unit or as a meaningful framework for comparative research? If so, we need to show that it is possible to delineate the 'external boundaries of the continent' and to demonstrate that 'the internal structure does not divide up into subdivisions which are unconnected or unrelated to each other' (Haller 1990).

At present there are two main reasons which suggest that Europe can be treated as a unit: increased economic interdependence between the different European states, and increased information exchange through the mass media as well as personal contact through tourism, study and work. At the same time it is also the case that these exchanges are intensifying at a global level. Perhaps the most significant factor to apply to Europe specifically is the increasing integration at a political level through agreements and treaties, and increasingly vigorous drives towards legislative and institutional standardization, particularly within the European Union (EU). But will increased integration within the EU act as a catalyst to greater homogeneity within Europe or will it exacerbate differences between EU members and non-members?

With the collapse of Soviet communism after 1989, market economies and liberal democracy have become dominant principles of organization for the whole of Europe, regardless of how long it might take for the former Soviet Bloc countries to implement these principles. However, this begs the question of whether such changes will result eventually in a significant levelling between eastern and western Europe or a more homogeneous and cohesive whole. A persistent factor of differentiation within Europe is the socio-economic level of development, as expressed not only in the per capita GNP but also in the 'quality of life' (standard of living, level of education, state of health, access to cultural facilities and life chances). So far, the various economic reforms and structural readjustment programmes carried out in the former Soviet bloc appear to have done little to ameliorate these differences (Brittan 1993).

There are also important historical and cultural differences which underlie the social organization of European societies, although there are some indications that these might be, if not receding, at least being attenuated. For example, with respect to religion it is possible to distinguish three major historical religious groupings: Catholic, Protestant and Orthodox Christianity. Linguistically, we can isolate three major groups: Romance, Germanic and Slavonic languages. Up to a point a correlation can be established between religion and language group, with the consequence that on the whole there is an overlap between Catholicism and Romance languages, between Protestantism and Germanic languages and Orthodoxy and Slavonic languages. To what extent we can establish other correlations, between say Protestantism, liberalism and economic development (Weber 1930; MacFarlane 1978) and say Orthodoxy, authoritarianism and economic underdevelopment (with Catholicism somewhere in between) is open to discussion (Haller 1990). Indeed, these linguistic and religious divisions are often seen to underlie the major ethnic cleavages and conflicts in contemporary Europe, from Northern Ireland and Belgium, to Bosnia and the Balkans (see Ruane, chapter 6 and Bowman, chapter 7, this volume).

Some anthropologists suggest that correlations can be made between 'anthropological phenomena' such as religion, family form and political orientation (see Todd 1985).[16] This proposition is problematic, but does nevertheless encourage a broader understanding of European societies and a historical perspective, without which the context in which these phenomena occur cannot be meaningfully grasped.

Answers to the question of 'what is Europe' hinge, in many respects, upon the problematic issues of classification and definition; yet these in turn are not only problems of semantics but of ideology and politics. Indeed, the concept of 'Europe' has been used and misused, and interpreted or misinterpreted from so many different perspectives that its meanings appear to be both legion and contradictory. This is not surprising, given that definitions of Europe are frequently both arbitrary and politically charged. There are interesting parallels here with the idea of nation. As Gervais (1993) points out in his study of England and 'Englishness' in

16. See the interesting discussion of differences within Europe explained along the lines of religion and family by E. Todd, 'Las Tres Claves de la Modernidad', E. Todd, 'Las Fronteras de las Fronteras' and I. Kerkhofs, 'Valores y Cambio' in *El Pais*, 25 January 1993, special edition 'Europa: el nuevo continente'.

literature, every image of 'the nation' is inescapably partial – a highly selective and edited version of that elusive whole, tailored for specific audiences and a particular end. Like the nation-state (against which it is often identified), 'Europe' can be seen as much as a creation of literature and myth as it is of power. Indeed, as Foucault's work on the relationship between knowledge, power and the rise of institutions illustrates, these elements are historically rather closely connected.

What is particularly interesting to note, both historically and sociologically, is the way in which the 'idea of Europe' as a political ideal and mobilizing metaphor has become increasingly prominent in the latter part of the twentieth century. Much of the catalyst behind this has undoubtedly been the the movement towards economic and legal union among the states of western and southern Europe. The growth of the European Union has rendered even more urgent and problematic the question of defining Europe. One effect of this, which has increased *pari passu* with the advance towards the millennium, has been a growing number of speeches and books by European leaders and intellectuals setting out their 'visions' of Europe. On closer inspection, however, what appears to be the voice of prophecy often turns out to be one of expediency. As Shore and Black observe, Article 237 of the Treaty of Rome states that 'any European country is eligible for membership to the EC', yet it fails to specify what 'European' means for countries outside the EC. Given the perceived economic and political advantages of membership, it clearly matters to some governments on which side of the 'European/non-European' divide their country falls.

To some extent, therefore, 'Europe' might be considered an example of what Turner called a 'master symbol': an icon that embraces a whole spectrum of different referents and meanings. But 'Europe' is also a discourse of power: a configuration of knowledge shaped by political and economic institutions that are themselves embedded in the disciplines and practices of government. Moreover, it is a discourse that has increasingly been appropriated by the European Community as a shorthand for itself. However vague or ill-defined the concept, to be 'European' or 'in favour of Europe' is increasingly taken to mean support for the European Community and its goal of 'ever-closer union'.

To see Europe in terms of discourses of power is simply to remind oneself that definitions are not always neutral, objective or disinterested. It also draws our attention to the power relations between observer and observed that such classifications often entail. Wallace (1990) illustrates this point cogently in his analysis of the different ways in which Europe has been defined in recent years. Here the boundaries of 'Europe' shift according to whether it is defined in terms of institutional structures, historical geography, or observed patterns of social, economic and political interaction. In each case, a different 'core' area emerges. Yet more problematic still is Wallace's emphasis on the importance of Europe as a distinctive cultural entity, one united by 'shared values, culture and psychological identity' (1990: 9–10). Advocates of this kind of 'cultural approach' point to Europe's heritage of classical Graeco–Roman civilization, Christianity, the ideas of the Enlightenment, and the triumph of Science, Reason, Progress and Democracy as the key markers of this shared European legacy. Significantly, these are all features which European Community officials emphasize as being particularly representative of 'the European idea' as they see it (Shore and Black, this volume, chapter 13; see also Shore 1993). There are also definitions of Europe which involve a subtext of racial and cultural chauvinism, particularly when confronted with Islam. For some, therefore, the definition and meaning of 'Europe' acquires saliency only when pitted against that which is 'non-European'.

If there is something that we can call Europe, understood perhaps as an ideal type, what characteristics does it exhibit? According to Zettenberg (1991) there are several self-regulating and autonomous institutions, associated with specific key values and types of freedom, which can be used to describe modern Europe. For Zettenberg, the economy is associated with prosperity and free trade; government with order and civic liberties; science with knowledge and academic freedom; religion with sacredness and religious tolerance; arts with beauty and artistic licence and ethics with virtue and the right to follow one's own conscience. The problem with these sets of correlations is that they are historical and conjunctural. Thus they apply elsewhere (notably the US), and have not at all times applied to what in other contexts we might consider to be European countries (were Spain under Franco, Italy under Mussolini, Greece under the Junta not *European* for the duration of these regimes?) As sets of ideals or aspirations they might well be at the forefront of European culture, as well as other national cultures, but they are not effective markers of the boundaries of Europe.

The Future of Europe and The Future of an Anthropology of Europe

The close of the twentieth century represents a momentous period in the history of Europe, but at present we can only have a hazy picture of what is likely to emerge in the future. As social scientists we have had to confront major international events: the collapse of Communism in eastern Europe, the end of the Cold War, increasing integration of the economies of the European Union, the breakdown of Yugoslavia and protracted war throughout Bosnia. We have simultaneously witnessed prolonged economic recession and mass unemployment, as well as increasing right-wing violence throughout eastern and western Europe. Yet we face these phenomena often bereft of suitable anthropological categories. Although many 'classical' anthropologists have contributed to the issues of nationality and nationalism (see Llobera, chapter 4, and Ruane, chapter 6, this volume), anthropology as a whole has been limited by its emphasis on small-scale units. Where progress has been made, largely through profitable exchanges with sociologists and social historians, this has been limited to developments appropriate only to the national state.

In the present circumstances, at a time of incessant change, the danger we face is that our short-term analyses may be dated by the time of their publication. Yet medium-term and long-term projections are difficult to muster when no clear trends seem to emerge. Tilly (1992), a leading historical sociologist, envisages a number of possible scenarios concerning the future of Europe. In the short term he predicts two different trends. Firstly, the proliferation of states matching the more bellicose and/or diplomatically successful populations that at present lack states of their own. This trend applies particularly to eastern Europe. Secondly, he sees the continuation of the long-term trend towards the consolidation into a decreasing number of more or less homogeneizing states; at the limit we are talking about a vast single European Community, with increased state-like powers and a certain sense of cultural identity.

However, in the long run Tilly sees the most important feature as the detachment of the principle of cultural distinctiveness from that of statehood. The implication of this is the creation of a strongly connected but multicultural Europe in which most individuals function bilingually (or trilingually) and exercise their right to territorial mobility in pursuit of opportunities and preferences. It also implies that the desire of ethno-nations to claim national independence within the framework of separate states will greatly diminish, because the European Union will offer all the advantages of being a free nation without the costs and inconvenience of being an independent state. The existing states, in whichever form they may exist, will cease to enforce cultural homogeneity and political dominance within their domain.

Tilly is well aware that this outlook may seem too optimistic given the lessons from history. That is why he allows for the possibility of two variants which might be realized within the long-term: a benign development, characterized by pluralism and diversity and with an absence of squabbles and attempts at domination, and a malign version, characterized by segmentation, hatred and parochialism, in the context of gross inequalities and violent ethnic conflicts.

All these possible developments identified by Tilly have relevance to the anthropological agenda for the future, concerned as they are with the interconnections between culture, identity and institutional frameworks. Our ability to meet the challenges of the future depends on our capacity to elaborate appropriate frameworks and concepts.

It is important that, while capitalizing on anthropology's ethnographic expertise, bringing awareness of local realities and grass-roots reactions, we expand our repertoire to enable fruitful systematic comparative analysis. Anthropologists have wrestled for generations with the problem of relating the local to the national or the global, and the temptation to succumb to the merits of the micro-study has frequently been overwhelming. But it is essential to persevere not only in locating the local within its wider context but in tackling the very institutions and practices which define and constitute the national and the supra-national levels in question. A historical dimension is important here not only in terms of coming to grips with the nature and shape of groups and institutions, but also in defining the overall object of study itself: that is, 'Europe'.

If Europe is considered as a unit, there follow a number of questions. For example, what are the political, cultural and economic consequences of mass immigration on Europe? What are the effects of global culture, particularly in the mass media, on European national cultures? How is increasing contact through tourism affecting traditional stereotypes about different European national and ethnic groups? We should also consider the impact of the global economy and the strategies of European and non-European transnational corporations, and the extent to which these might shape national and EU policies. Furthermore, what are the effects of the process of European integration on national identity and state sovereignty? Are there any institutions or policies which are helping to generate a European consciousness?

Given that 'Europe' itself is a disputed category, and yet one that has a bearing on many aspects of people's lives, one contribution of anthropology from an ethnographic point of view might be the exploration of what Europe means to different groups and individuals, and the many ways in which they conceptualize or talk about Europe in relation to their own identity. This is one of the themes that runs through a number of the contributions to this volume (Mandel; Chapman; Bowman; Ruane). If it is the *experience* of Europe that interests us, or Europe as a source of *identity* (Garcia 1993), then we need to be sensitive to the many different ways that this experience is mediated through other social factors such as religion, class, ethnicity, nationality and gender. In this respect, to speak of a single, all-constitutive 'Europe' becomes rather meaningless, or worse, encourages an essentialized vision of Europeanness as a quality that is somehow fixed, bounded, homogeneous and pure. Instead, we should recognize the plurality and diversity of the many different Europes that exist, and have existed, in any given time or context, and the ways in which these different meanings might be deployed to different effect. The way to see the different 'Europes' is as cultural conceptions advanced by diverse groups competing for hegemony in the political arena. This does not exclude the acknowledgment that some visions are more dominant than others.

The Scope of This Volume

The articles included in this volume originated from a conference held at Goldsmiths College, University of London, in June 1992 under the title 'The Anthropology of Europe: After 1992'. The aim of the conference was to explore old paradigms and new directions in European social anthropology, particularly in the areas of ethnicity, nationalism and gender. The implications of European unification both for the organization of European societies and for European anthropology were central themes underlying conference debates. Indeed the contributions to this volume reflect these concerns and in many ways represent a departure from conventional anthropological perspectives.

What many chapters have in common is an attempt to chart new research directions in European social anthropology in response to the changing character of European societies. Taking up the criticisms of European anthropology that were first highlighted by Boissevain and others in the 1970s, many contributors attempt to grapple with larger-scale social processes, including nationalism, migration, European Community institutions and state policy. Boissevain's chapter identifies three inter-related developments currently taking place that he suggests will feature prominently in anthropological research during the next few decades: changing patterns of production, movements of people and nostalgia for a sense of identity perceived as being eroded as a result of modernity and globalization. The theme of identity and boundaries and the relationship between migrants, conceptions of national identity and citizenship, is examined by Mandel, drawing on her ethnographic study of Turks in Berlin. Mandel argues that definitions of citizenship in Germany are conflated with notions of ethnicity and race, which produce and legitimize the category of outsider or *Auslander*.

Garcia explores the question of what it means to be a 'citizen' at national and supranational levels, arguing that Spain lags behind its European partners in terms of the rights and entitlements of its citizens. This she attributes to the history of the Spanish state and its weak relationship with 'civil society'. She draws an interesting parallel with the European Union, where there is also a problem of a lack of popular democratic participation. Attempts by the EU to create such a European citizenship are analysed by Shore and Black. As they show, a new iconography has been invented to lend legitimacy to the political aspirations of European Union institutions, but the reality of a 'citizen's Europe' has yet to be achieved.

The tension between the European Union and the member states is a theme that recurs in several chapters. Llobera's paper explores the contributions of Van Gennep and Mauss to the study of nationalism in Europe in the aftermath of the First World War. Many of the issues at stake, and particularly the impact of the principle of self-determination in multinational states and empires, are still relevant today, particularly in the light of the collapse of the Soviet Union and Yugoslavia.

Ruane argues that European integration is often perceived as heralding the end of the age of nationalism in Europe, yet nationalist concerns seem to have been incorporated into the very framework of the EU. This challenges the view of a post-nationalist Europe. Focusing on the Irish Republic, Ruane highlights the importance of nationalist ideologies and discourses and their implications for the future of Europe.

The boundaries of the new Europe are a problem explored by Chapman. Focusing on Poland, and the related questions of capital movements, trade barriers and the 'nationality' of transnational corporations, he illustrates some of the difficulties in establishing clear frontiers between the EU and non-community Europe, and the implications for those countries excluded from the Union.

If Ruane, Chapman, Shore and Black and others are concerned with the formation of a European state, Bowman explores the breakdown of a former federal state: Yugoslavia. Using a Lacanian perspective, he tries to explain the rise of ethnic hatred and violence that has come to epitomize the conflict in that country. For Bowman, ambiguity over ethnic and territorial boundaries, combined with the breakdown of authority (understood in a psychological as well as a political sense) has resulted in what many see as a descent into barbarism. From the perspective of the EU there is a temptation to disassociate the new republics from the project of Europeanism.

The problematic nature of national identities is also explored by Stanton in connection with Gibraltar's contradictory status as an outpost of the now defunct British Empire. As Stanton suggests, in a post-colonial world, becoming European poses problems for the Gibraltarians' already contradictory identity. The contradictions of this identity are to do with British identity, which is intrinsically linked to the concept and experience of empire. The question that emerges with the collapse of the British Empire is the content and meaning of being British and the disjunction between geopolitics and the remnants of a 'mirage of empire'.

In a different context, O'Brien explores the multiple identities which exist in a French Catalonian village. Her study illustrates the contextual nature of social identities, pointing out not only that women are more influential than men in reproducing ethnic identity, but also that they tend to shift towards a Catalan identity as they grow older. In fact, gender has been an important element in anthropological research in some areas of Europe, notably through studies focused on 'honour and shame'. But this framework has met with growing criticism, and its limitations in terms of providing a basis for comparative study have become increasingly obvious. Comas' contribution to this volume explores the advantages of an alternative framework to the comparative study of gender in Europe, based on a consideration of 'support and care'. She considers the sexual division of labour and the ideological elaboration of masculinity and femininity in rural and urban areas of Spain, arguing that these must be understood in relation to state policies and welfare provisions. The importance of linking local practices and beliefs with wider national and supranational levels of determination is further explored by Goddard. While on the one hand recognizing the importance of a historical and global contextualization of anthropological work, Goddard argues that a careful appraisal of (Mediterranean and non-Mediterranean) European anthropology offers important inroads into the development of a comparative study of European societies. Both Comas and Goddard emphasize the importance of studying gender, not only to explain inequalities between men and women, but because gender divisions are relevant to the production and reproduction of other encompassing manifestations of social difference.

Although this collection does not represent a coherent proposal for future work in European anthropology, our aim has been to explore, via critique and innovation, possible avenues for research. Although a number of different avenues would be beneficial to the discipline as a whole, we do argue for proposals that are cognizant of the importance of a historical approach and sensitive to the implications of national and global processes. The question of methodology is relevant here. Whilst recognizing the contribution of fieldwork and related techniques, we propose that anthropologists must broaden their methodological repertoire in order to grasp the complexities of history and of global determinations. Here an interdisciplinary approach would seem to be invaluable. Anthropologists working in Europe ignore at their peril the qualitative and quantitative methodologies offered by sociology and history. Blok (1992) suggests that anthropologists are generally unfamiliar with the methods, models and contributions of historians. And yet anthropologists would benefit from cross-fertilization with this discipline, which recognizes different levels theorization of the social and cultural spectrum, from microunits to macrounits (Tilly 1990). Similarly, if we take the case of sociology, of the introductions to three recent collections on the anthropology of Europe – Pina-Cabral (1992), Hastrup (1992) and MacDonald (1993) – only MacDonald makes mention of sociological texts. Historical sociology in particular has in the past twenty-five years made an outstanding contribution to explaining how European modernity came into being – a concern that would be central to the anthropology of Europe. But what would be the anthropologist's specific contribution to the study of European (and indeed other contemporary) societies?

It has been frequently stated that anthropological work is defined by its research technique, that is, participant observation in a face-to-face situation (traditionally in a small community). If anthropology often appears as just the sum of its ethnographies, and the knowledge of higher-level socio-cultural units (be they districts, regions, ethnonations, nation-states, multinational states, federations, world-system or wider social and cultural manifestations and traits) is problematic and approached with diffidence, this is largely a consequence of the limitations imposed by the centrality of this research technique.

What might have made sense among the Trobrianders and Tikopians of yesteryear is inadequate in relation to the Piedmontese or Bretons of today (not to speak of the European Union bureaucrats or transnational corporations). The issue here is that anthropologists should not be defined by their adherence to a specific way of collecting data, but by the scientific character of their projects. The question is not whether the anthropologist should or should not embark on fieldwork, but that the latter should not be the *fons et origo* of the discipline.

The legacy of the discipline is an acute sensitivity among its practitioners to the complexity and contradictory nature of social processes. Anthropologists are well aware of the specificities which global economic processes or wide-ranging ideologies may acquire for particular groups or localities. At the same time, they are well equipped to contextualize local beliefs and practices within a wider comparative framework, thus undermining any claims of universality that might underlie such beliefs and practices. Anthropologists have historically been concerned with those social groups or conditions which have for one reason or another been rendered 'peripheral' (Nugent 1988). They have often been the sole mediators for those rendered powerless and voiceless, although their role here has been scrutinized and – quite rightly – criticized. While taking on board these critiques, this continues to be an urgent task for the discipline, whether in the periphery of the world system or the peripheralized groups within Europe. At the same time, anthropologists have become intent on applying their skills to the study of those organizations and ideologies which may indeed have a hand in reproducing peripheralization, but whose main objective is to reproduce existing power structures, or indeed invent new ones. Thus anthropologists have before them a rich and varied field and a challenging and important task.

References

Ahmed, A. S. (1976). *Millennium and Charisma among Pathans*, London: RKP.

Almond, G. and Verba, S. (1963). *The Civic Culture. Political Attitudes and Democracy in Five Nations*, Princeton: Princeton University Press.

Arensberg, C. M. (1963). The Old World Peoples: The Place of European Cultures in World Ethnography. *Anthropological Quarterly*, **36**, (3), 75–99.

Asad, T. (1972). Market model, class structure and consent: a reconsideration of Swat political organisation. *Man*, **7**, (1), 74–94.

Bailey, F. (ed.) (1971). *Gifts and Poison: The Politics of Reputation*, Oxford: Blackwell.

Bailey, F. (ed.) (1973). *Debate and Compromise. The Politics of Innovation*, Oxford: Blackwell.

Banfield, E. (1958). *The Moral Basis of Backward Society*, New York: Free Press.

Banton, M. (ed.) (1966). *Social Anthropology of Complex Societies*, ASA Monograph 4, London: Tavistock.

Barnes, J. A. (1954). Class and Committees in a Norwegian Island Parish. *Human Relations*, **7**, (1), 39–58.

Barnes, J. A. (1972). *Networks in Social Anthropology*, Reading.

Barth, F. (1959). *Political Leadership Among the Swat Pathan*, London: The Athlone Press.

Barth, F. (1966). *Models of Social Organisation*, Occasional Paper No.

23, London: RAI.
Barth, F. (1969). *Ethnic Groups and Boundaries: The Social Organisation of Cultural Difference*, London: Allen & Unwin.
Benedict, R. (1946a). *Patterns of Culture*, NY: Penguin.
Benedict, R. (1946b). *The Chrysanthemum and the Sword*, Boston: Houghton Mifflin.
Blok, A. (1974). *The Mafia of a Sicilian Village*, Oxford: Blackwell.
Blok, A. (1981). Rams and Billy Goats: A Key to the Mediterranean Code of Honor. *Man*, **16**, (3), 427–40.
Blok, A. (1992). Reflections on Making History. In *Other Histories* (ed. K. Hastrup), London: Routledge.
Boissevain, J. (1966). Patronage in Sicily. *Man*, **2**, 18–33.
Boissevain, J. (1968). The Place of Non-groups in the Social Sciences. *Man*, **3/4**, 542–56.
Boissevain, J. (1969). *Hal Farug. A Village in Malta*, New York: Holt, Reinhart and Winston.
Boissevain, J. (1974). *Friends of Friends: Networks, Manipulators and Coalitions*, Oxford: Blackwell.
Boissevain, J. (1976). Uniformity and Diversity in the Mediterranean. In *Kinship and Modernisation* (ed. J. Peristany), pp. 1–11, Rome: Center for Mediterranean Studies.
Boissevain, J. (1977). Towards a Social Anthropology of Europe. In *Beyond the Community: Social Processes in Europe* (ed. J. Boissevain and J. Friedl), pp. 9–17, The Hague: Department of Education and Science, The Netherlands.
Boissevain, J. and Blok, A. (1974). Western Mediterranean Folk Cultures, *Encyclopaedia Britannica*, 15th edn, **2**, 852–4.
Bott, E. (1955). Urban Families: Conjugal Roles and Social Relations. *Human Relations*, **8**, (4), 345–84.
Bott, E. (1957). *Family and Social Networks*, London: Tavistock.
Brittan, S. (1993). Economic Viewpoint: The Painful Road to Capitalism. *Financial Times*, 30 September, p.18.
Campbell, J. K. (1964). *Honour, Family and Patronage. A Study of Institutions and Moral Values in a Greek Mountain Community*, Oxford: Clarendon Press.
Cole, J. (1977). Anthropology Comes Part-Way Home. *Annual Review of Anthropology*, **6**, 349–378.
Crockatt, R. (1987). The Cold War, Past and Present. In *The Cold War, Past and Present* (eds R. Crockatt and S. Smith) pp. 3–23, London: Allen & Unwin.
Cuisinier, J. (1993). *Ethnologie de l'Europe*, Paris: PUF.

Cuisinier, J. and Segalen, M. (1993). *Ethnologie de la France*. Paris: PUF.

Cutileiro, J. (1971). *A Portuguese Rural Society*, Oxford: Clarendon Press and OUP.

Davis, J. (1977). *People of the Mediterranean: An Essay in Comparative Social Anthropology*, London: RKP.

Dubisch, J. (1983). Greek Women, Sacred or Profane. In Women and Men in Greece: a society in transition (eds Mackrakis and Allen). *Journal of Modern Greek Studies*, **1**, (1).

Du Boulay, J. (1974). *Portrait of a Greek Mountain Village*, Oxford: Clarendon Press.

Du Boulay, J. (1978). The Greek Vampire: a study of cyclic symbolism in marriage and death. *Man*, (NS) **17**, 219–38.

Foster, G. M. (1965). Peasant Society and the Image of Limited Good. *American Anthropologist*, **67**, (2).

Foster, G. M. (1973) [1962]. *Traditional Societies and Technological Change*, (2nd edn). NY: Harper and Row. First published in 1962 as *Traditional Cultures and the Impact of Technological Change*.

Freeman, S. (1973). Introduction to European Social Organisation. *American Anthropologist*, **75**, 743–50.

Friedl, E. (1958). Hospital Care in Provincial Greece. *Human Organization*, **16**, (40), 24–7.

Friedl, E. (1959). The Role of Kinship in the Transmission of National Culture to Rural Villages of Mainland Greece. *American Anthropologist*, **61**, 30–8.

Friedl, E. (1962). *Vasilika*, New York: Holt, Rinehart and Winston.

Garcia, S. (ed.) (1993). *European Identity and the Search for Legitimacy*. London: Pinter.

Gellner, E. and Waterbury, J. (eds) (1977). *Patrons and Clients*, London: Duckworth.

Gervais, D. (1993). *Literary Englands: 'Versions of Englishness' in Modern Writing*, Cambridge: Cambridge University Press.

Gilmore, D. (1977). Patronage and Class Conflict in Southern Spain. *Man*, **12**, 446–58.

Gilmore, D. (1982). Anthropology of the Mediterranean Area. *Annual Review of Anthropology*, **11**, 175–207.

Gilmore, D. (ed.) (1987). Introduction to *Honour and Shame and the Unity of the Mediterranean*, Washington: American Ethnological Association.

Goddard, V. (1986). Honour and Shame: The Control of Women's Sexuality and Group Identity in Naples. In *The Cultural*

Construction of Sexuality (ed. P. Caplan), London: Routledge.
Goffman, I. (1959). *The Presentation of Self in Everyday Life*, New York: Doubleday.
Grillo, R. D. (ed.) (1980). *'Nation' and 'State' in Europe. Anthropological Perspectives*, London: Academic Press.
Haller, M. (1990). The Challenge for Contemporary Sociology in the Transformation of Europe. *International Sociology*, **5**, 183–204.
Hastrup, K. (1992). *Other Histories*. London: Routledge.
Herzfeld, M. (1981). Meaning and Morality: A Semiotic Approach to Evil Eye Accusations in a Greek Village. *American Ethnologist*, **8**, 560–74.
Herzfeld, M. (1987). *Anthropology Through the Looking-Glass*, Cambridge: Cambridge University Press.
Hirschon, R. (1978). Open Body/Closed Space: the transformation of female sexuality. In *Defining Females* (ed. S. Ardener), London: Croom Helm.
Jackson, A. (ed.) (1985). *Anthropology at Home*, London: Tavistock.
Kapferer, B. (ed.) (1976). *Transaction and Meaning: Directions in the Anthropology of Exchange and Symbolic Behaviour*, Philadelphia: Inst. for the Study of Human Issues.
Kay, C. (1989). *Latin American Theories of Development and Underdevelopment*, London: Macmillan.
Kenny, M. (1963). Europe: The Atlantic Fringe. *Anthropological Quarterly*, **36**, (3), 100–19.
Kenny M. and Kertzer, D. (eds) (1983). *Urban Life in Mediterranean Europe: Anthropological Perspectives*, Urbana and Chicago: University of Illinois Press.
Llobera, J. R. (1986). Fieldwork in Southwestern Europe, *Critique of Anthropology*, **6**, (2), 25–33.
Llobera, J. R. (1993). Reconstructing Anthropology: the task for the nineties. In *Despues de Malinowski* (ed. J. Besterd), Tenerife: Actas del VI Congreso de Antropologia.
Lowie, R. H. (1954). *Toward Understanding Germany*. Chicago: Chicago University Press.
MacDonald, S. (ed.) (1993). *Inside European Identities*, Oxford: Berg.
MacFarlane, A. (1978). *The Origins of English Individualism. The Family, Property and Social Transition*, Oxford: Blackwell.
Magnarella, P. (1993). Conceptualising the Circum-Mediterranean, *Journal of Mediterranean Studies*, **2**, (1), 18–24.
Nugent, S. (1988). The Peripheral Situation, *Annual Review of Anthropology*, **17**, 79–98.

Okely, J. (1977). Gypsy Women: models in conflict. In *Perceiving Women* (ed. S. Ardener), London: Croom Helm.

Ott, S. (1981). *The Circle of Mountains*, Oxford: Clarendon Press.

Parsons, A. (1967). Is the Oedipus Complex Universal? A South Italian "nuclear complex". In *Personalities and Culture* (ed. R. Hunt), Austin, Texas: University Press. 352–99.

Peristiany, J. G. (1974) [1966]. *Honour and Shame. The Values of Mediterranean Society*, Medway Reprint; originally printed in Chicago: Chicago University Press.

Pina-Cabral, J. (1989). The Mediterranean as a Category of Cultural Comparison. *Current Anthropology*, **30**, 399–406.

Pina-Cabral, J. (1992). Against Translation. In *Europe Observed* (eds J. Pina-Cabral and J. Campbell), 1–23, London: Macmillan.

Pitkin, D. S. (1963). Mediterranean Europe. *Anthropological Quarterly*, **36**, (3), 120–9.

Pitt-Rivers, J. (1963). Mediterannean Countrymen: *Essays in the Social Anthropology of the Mediterannean*, Paris/The Hague: Mouton.

Pitt-Rivers, J. (1966). Honour and Social Status. In (1974 [1966]) *Honour and Shame. The Values of Mediterranean Society* (ed. J. G. Peristiany), Chicago: Chicago University Press.

Pitt-Rivers, J. (1971) [1954]. *The People of the Sierra*, (2nd edn), Chicago and London: University of Chicago Press. First published 1954, London: Weidenfeld & Nicholson.

Redfield, R. (1971) [1956]. *Peasant Society and Culture: an anthropological approach to civilization*, Chicago: Chicago University Press.

Redfield, R. (1973) [1960]. *The Little Community. Peasant Society and Culture*, Chicago: Chicago University Press.

Schneider, J. and Schneider, P. (1976). *Culture and Political Economy in Western Sicily*, London and New York: Academic Press.

Segalen, M. (ed.) (1989). *L' autre et le semblable. Regards sur l'ethnologie des sociétés contemporaines*, Paris: Editions du CNRS.

Shore, C. (1990). *Italian Communism. The Escape from Leninism: an anthropological perspective*, London: Pluto Press.

Shore, C. (1993). Inventing the "People's Europe": critical perspectives on European Community "cultural policies". *Man. Journal of the Royal Anthropological Institute*, **28**, (4), 779–800.

Tilly, C. (1990). Future History. In *Interpreting the Past, Understanding the Present* (eds S. Kendrick and D. McCrone), London: Macmillan.

Tilly, C. (1992). The Future of European States, *Social Research*, **59**, (40), 705–18.

Wallace, W. (1990). *The Transformation of Europe*, London: Pinter.

Weber, M. (1930). *The Protestant Ethic and the Spirit of Capitalism*, London: Allen & Unwin.

White, C. (1980). *Patrons and Partisans: A Study of Two Southern Italian Comuni*, Cambridge: Cambridge University Press.

Wolf, E. (1966a). *Peasants*. Englewood Cliffs, NJ: Prentice-Hall.

Wolf, E. (1966b). Kinship, friendship and patron–client relationships in complex societies. In *The Social Anthropology of Complex Societies* (ed. M. Banton), pp. 1–22, London: Tavistock.

Zettenberg, H. (1991). The Structuration of Europe. *Journal of Public Opinion Research*, **394**, 309–12.

Chapter 2

Towards an Anthropology of European Communities?[1]

Jeremy Boissevain

Current social developments in Europe are increasing the total number of its constituent communities. As these communities seek to establish and defend their identities, there is growing political, economic and symbolic activity within and between them. This paper points to some of the developments that may well be overlooked in the rush to assess the impact on anthropology of the European Community. It also suggests some of the ways these may influence theoretical developments in the social anthropology of Europe.

Changing Theoretical Interests

Twenty years ago a number of social and cultural anthropologists working in Europe were turning away from functionalist-inspired community studies, which, by their narrow village-centred approach, were tribalizing Europe. While retaining the local-level base, these new studies began to move beyond individual communities in an attempt to understand the configurations they formed with higher levels of integration (cf. Bax 1976; Blok 1974; Boissevain and Friedl 1975; Schneider and Schneider 1976; Verrips 1977, 1980). Many of the studies from this period were down-to-earth monographs which dealt with specific political and economic themes from a historical perspective focused on power relations.

1. I am grateful to Gerard Hersbach and Cris Shore for helpful comments on an earlier draft of the present discussion.

Generally, they paid relatively less attention to ritual or symbolic activities.

A decade later, in the 1980s, a significant shift in interest was evident. Often focusing on ritual, many studies were concerned with the analysis of symbolism and symbolic behaviour (cf. Cohen 1982, 1985, 1986). I do not intend to explore here the epistemology of the shift in focus from the social to the cultural and cognitive, that is, why much of social anthropology has become cultural anthropology. Other contributors will address these questions. It no doubt has much to do with the charisma and power of leading anthropologists who had largely given up fieldwork to focus on myth, ritual, pollution and the Bible: Claude Lévi-Strauss, Edmund Leach, Mary Douglas, Clifford Geertz and Victor Turner. Be that as it may, the change in accent is also related to other influences.

Theoretical shifts are not only influenced by great teachers. They also reflect developments in the societies in which theoreticians live. Although Firth (1954) and Leach (1954) by the early 1950s had begun questioning the value of structural-functionalism in interpreting their own field data, the demise of this theoretical paradigm was hastened by its inability to provide adequate insights into the anti-colonial revolts and class-based conflicts prominent during the late 1950s and 1960s. But in spite of Kuhn's work (1970), the influence of social processes on theoretical developments is still often ignored, and shifts in theoretical focus are attributed solely to academic debate. The influence on debate of developments in the society in which that intellectual activity takes place is largely ignored.

For example, Victor Turner, in his postlude to Manning's 1983 collection, *The Celebration of Society*, asked, 'But why, I repeat, have anthropologists, folklorists, . . . begun, of late, to flock to the field of ludic studies?' (1983a: 188). His answer was that, finally, anthropologists had begun to see the light: 'It is gradually being brought home to us that we have been in error, in "bracketing off" such celebrations as "mystification," "false consciousness," "lower stages of cultural evolution," "ideological confusion," and similar pejorative evaluations based on consciousness of our own cognitive superiority' (ibid.: 190–1).

He thus suggested that the change in focus was the result of a process internal to the community of scholars conceived as an isolate. But at the same time that this theoretical shift was taking place, a revitalization of pilgrimages and public celebrations was occurring throughout Europe, not to mention Asia, Africa and the Americas (Manning 1983; Boissevain 1992). Though Turner was well aware of these developments (1974: 210, 211, 223; 1983b: 110, 112, 124 n.2), it does not seem to have occurred to him that the growing attention to ludic celebrations could also have been stimulated by the increasing number of such festivities in the societies in which the anthropologists and folklorists lived and worked.

Shifts in scientific paradigms cannot be fully understood unless they are examined against the social fabric of the societies in which they occur. The shift from social to cultural anthropology, from post-structural-functional transactionalism and political economy to symbolism and deconstruction, was related to social developments that were occurring outside academe during the 1970s and 1980s. The shift in scholarly focus occurred at a time that there had been a long pause in the armed combat which had been endemic in western Europe. This peace, which permitted contemplation, proved conducive to the questioning of given authority, of the benefits of continuing industrial growth, of the effects of expanding communication possibilities, of the rapid globalization of culture. One of the consequences of this reflection and introspection was a revalorization of traditions abandoned in the post-Second World War rush for material prosperity. Ludic rituals and symbols that linked the present to an idealized pre-industrial life-style provided a sense of belonging and identity, and became increasingly important during the 1970s and 1980s (cf. Boissevain 1992; Hewison 1987).

In short, growing scholarly interest in the analysis of symbols and rituals, rather than exclusively the product of academic debate, was also a reflection of the growing general interest in ritual and symbolic activity in the societies in which anthropologists themselves lived and worked. Theoretical debate and paradigmatic shifts follow the outline of the underlying social reality of the societies in which they occur.

It follows that social developments taking place in Europe today will influence the anthropology of tomorrow. It is consequently useful to examine some of the social processes affecting contemporary European societies.

Three interrelated developments are taking place that I think will influence the activities of anthropologists working on Europe during the next decade or so. These are the changing patterns of production, the movement of peoples and the nostalgia to which I have already alluded.

Changing Production

During the past two decades there has been a marked change in patterns of economic activity that has challenged the dominant position of West European manufacturers. The increase in production costs following the energy crisis of the mid-1970s led to the transfer to developing countries of many low-skilled (and often polluting) production processes. In addition, consumers, for various reasons (including the growth of more sophisticated advertising and the media), became increasingly dissatisfied with mass-produced, standard products and demanded varied and customized goods, for which they were willing to pay more. To meet this challenge, European manufacturers were obliged to produce more specialized, higher-quality products (Brusco 1982: 171; Sabel 1982: 199). This heralded what Charles Sabel has called the 'End of Fordism' (ibid.: 194–231), the end of the dominance of assembly-line production of goods destined for the mass market. Where Fordism centralized production, separated conception from execution and substituted unskilled for skilled labour, specialization required the opposite: decentralization, a reduction in scale and collaboration between designers and skilled producers. Unskilled labour became increasingly redundant. Miniaturization, computers and robots combined to produce massive lay-offs, not only in industry but also in labour-intensive white-collar sectors such as banking and publishing (see also Gershuny 1978).

These developments have resulted in the emergence in western Europe of an impoverished under-class of structurally un- or underemployed, many of whom are forming loose communities and developing distinctive subcultures. The alarming growth of this under-class has also been furthered by the dismantling of the costly welfare net put in place during the 1960s and 1970s. Aspects of these subcultures surface at weekends and at the solstices, when vandalism, violent racial xenophobia, joy-riding, the winter misery of the homeless and rituals at Stonehenge capture headlines. Respect for, if not the legitimacy of, European states is being weakened by their inability to provide a growing segment of their citizens with work, shelter and the level of benefits to which they

lslip Request 6/25/2016 2:42:46 PM

quest date:6/25/2016 01:54 PMRequest ID:401080
cation:LincPk Stacks
l Number:305.80094 A628g1994
n Barcode:
3 0 5 1 1 0 0 5 4 2 5 2 7 7

hor:
e: Anthropology of Europe : identity and boundaries in conflict / edited by Victoria A. Goddard, Josep R. Llobera, and Cris Shore.
umeration:c.1Year:
tron Name:ALICJA E KUBAS
tron Barcode:
2 0 5 1 1 1 3 4 7 8 8 5 0 0

assignment History:
ne

ail (if available):1501 TARA BELLE PKWY
tron comment:

ply to Reader: Item is not available...
At Bindery: Seeking next available
At Repair: Seeking next available
Brittle Review: Seeking next available
Item Charged Out: Seeking next available
Damaged: Seeking next available
Local Circulation Only: Seeking next available
Missing/ Not on Shelf: Seeking next available
Noncirculation Item: Seeking next available
On New Book Shelf

quest number:
4 0 1 0 8 0

ute to:
hare Library:
rary Pick Up Location:LPC CIRCULATION

have become accustomed.

Another consequence of changing modes of production is the growing awareness in Europe that there are strikingly different ways of doing much the same thing. Differences between Japanese and British automobile production have been discussed in the press. Less explored but equally fascinating questions include, for example: How were small family enterprises in Prato able to put the British reused woollen industry out of business (Boissevain 1984)? What exactly is the relation between kinship, share-cropping and the immensely successful high-technology cottage industries of central Italy that have made this region the wealthiest in the country (Bamford 1987)? Why are immigrants of Asian extraction generally more successful business entrepreneurs than Afro-Caribbean immigrants (Boissevain and Grotenbreg 1988; Ward 1988)?

Insiders and Outsiders: The Struggle for Identity

Even as long-established European nations integrate their economies, they are multiplying and becoming increasingly heterogeneous. At least two processes are responsible for this. First, European nation-states are losing their power to contain the struggle of minority groups for political identity. Second, everywhere there is movement of newcomers – immigrant labourers, refugees, tourists – into fairly homogeneous, settled communities. These developments are obviously not of the same order, but all establish populations of insiders and outsiders, and thus stimulate struggles for identity and the control of cultural and social boundaries.

Restive Minorities

The ethnic ferment in central and eastern Europe following the spectacular dissolution of the Communist regimes is a more recent powerful example of the inability of weakened states to control the identities and political ambitions of minorities. The fission of Yugoslavia, the Soviet Union and many of their constituent republics and provinces along ethnic fault-lines is creating new states. Their struggle to achieve statehood possibly will fuel aspirations for greater autonomy of west European minorities who have not yet been able to (re)gain political legitimacy. The struggles to divide social entities regarded as social and cultural wholes are bitter. They are causing massive population movements, as waves of new political refugees seek protection in western Europe, creating new groups of outsiders, and thus new boundaries to be defended.

Regional Ferment

The post-war period has been, at least for western Europe, a time of unprecedented peace and relative stability. For decades, the nation-states have not had to rally citizens against a common, outside enemy. Just as this stability furthered theoretical introspection, so it has also promoted localism by permitting the refocusing of attention and resources on rivals and boundaries closer to hand, on parochial and regional interests. This, in turn, has resulted in pressure for decentralization, for more regional autonomy. These regional movements have played an important part in stimulating the effervescence of public rituals as resources are channelled into local cultural manifestations. For example, in Andalusia there has been and explosive growth of the pilgrimage to the shrine of El Rocio, and in the Ladin-speaking area of the Italian Dolomites there has been a revitalization of carnival. Both events have become important vehicles of regional identity and cultural pride (Crain 1992; Poppi 1992).

Immigration

Other lines of cleavage are created by the continuing influx into western Europe of unskilled workers from Asia, the Mediterranean and Caribbean regions and, more recently, central and eastern Europe. Originally recruited as short-term 'guest workers' to fill positions on the lower rungs of the industrial ladder, many have now moved up a few rungs and been joined by their families. Western Europe has become an immigration destination. These immigrants have been disproportionatly affected by the structural unemployment. As their numbers and knowledge of how the system works have grown, so has their competition with the majority population for increasingly scarce jobs, welfare benefits and housing. This competition has furthered latent xenophobia and racism, which throughout Europe has become more open. The mounting, open racial violence in Germany during 1992 and 1993 has captured the headlines; but racial tension elsewhere in western Europe has also been rising as the stream of economic and political refugees grows.

Escalating ethnic unrest and overt racism is part of a vicious circle: it is aggravated by the inability of the states to redress the problem of structural unemployment which lies at the root of much of the discord. It is further exacerbated by the policy of most states to cut back on social benefits in order to stem budget deficits caused by rising welfare payments to growing numbers of unemployed. Furthermore, European Community treaties on immigration and minority groups and the European Convention on Human Rights have undermined the ability of EC states unilaterally to attack their minority populations by dealing severely with restive ethnic groups.

Rural and Urban Migrants

Another type of migration that creates strain, albeit of a different order, between established and outsider groups is the movement between urban and rural areas. During the 1950s and 1960s the rural poor moved to cities in search of (better-paid) work. At the same time, affluent urbanites began buying the rural cottages and farms vacated by the migrants for use as weekend homes. Beginning in the 1970s, increasing numbers began acquiring holiday/retirement houses farther away, in poor rural communities in Scandinavia, central France, Italy and elsewhere along the Mediterranean and, I suspect, more recently, in eastern Europe.

The friction and discrimination caused by the arrival of rural migrants in French, Italian and Spanish cities has been widely discussed. The effect of urban migrants on rural areas is less well documented (but see Brunt 1974). There are few studies of the impact of holiday-home owners (some exceptions are Esmeyer 1982; Gilligan 1987; Ireland 1987) or of the winter migration of growing numbers of less affluent elderly north Europeans to empty holiday accommodation in Spain and Malta. Nevertheless, the phenomenon of a second residence is widespread and growing.

For example, by 1984 in Gaiole in Chianti, one-third of the housing stock was owned by outsiders, mostly British and German but also Florentine and Roman (Verster 1985). In Malta, old 'character houses' vacated by villagers who have moved to new houses are being acquired by foreigners and wealthy Maltese townies in search of more tranquil and 'traditional' surroundings. Thus in many villages the core area is being slowly abandoned by natives and reoccupied and gentrified by wealthy outsiders who live next to natives who cannot afford to move (Boissevain 1986). If in Malta this has given rise to few incidents, arson attacks on holiday homes in Wales and Corsica demonstrate that the relations between locals and outside holiday-home owners can become fraught with tension.

Tourism

Ever-increasing hordes of tourists are streaming into the ancient cities, countryside and peripheral areas of Europe. In 1990, some 187 million tourists travelled to West European countries. Of these visitors, more than eight out of ten came from other European countries. (See Table 2.1. Owing to the unavailability of comparable statistics, the table underrepresents the totals, since it does not include Scandinavian destinations and often shows arrivals at accommodation rather than at frontiers). It is clear, however, that hundreds of millions of outsiders are annually entering, lodging in and exploring European countries. Each year their numbers increase.

The motives that impel tourists to undertake costly and sometimes gruelling journeys are hotly debated. Some see the tourist as a contemporary pilgrim fleeing the superficiality of modern society in a quest for 'authenticity' (MacCannell 1976). Others view tourists as engaged in a sacred journey to a world free from the constraints of work, time and conformity, a ludic interlude that renews the traveller to be able to cope again with the strictures and structures of everyday life (Graburn 1977). It is obvious, I think, that it is not possible to attribute a single motive to the millions of tourists. They have different motives and, globally speaking, their tastes are changing. Just as consumers became increasingly dissatisfied with standard, mass-produced goods, and demanded more varied and customized products, so today's tourists are rejecting standard mass package tours. More and more are seeking individualized holidays that cater for their desire for learning, nostalgia, heritage, and for a closer look at the Other. Not sun, sea and sand, but culture and nature have become the objects of the post-modern post-tourist (Urry 1990).

Regardless of their motives, tourists are outsiders who penetrate established communities for short periods and impinge upon indigenous populations. In some places tourist curiosity has fostered an awareness of local culture. In Malta, for example, tourist interest in parish celebrations has helped to make these

Table 2.1: 1990 Tourist Arrivals at European Frontiers

Country	Total Arrivals	Market Share from Europe %	Change in Total Arrivals 1989–1990 %
Austria*	19,011,397	87.76	4.4
Cyprus	1,600,170	82.23**	10.3
France	53,157,000	83.36	5.9
Germany*	15,626,858	68.55	6.6
Gr. Britain***	18,021,000	60.42	3.9
Greece	8,873,310	88.92	9.8
Ireland	3,666,000	84.53	5.2
Italy*	20,862,965	74.08	1.4
Luxembourg*	820,476	91.10	–6.1
Malta	871,675	90.91	5.2
Netherlands*	5,795,100	80.94	11.3
Portugal	8,019,919	92.56	12.7
Spain*	12,251,352	84.91	–12.2
Switzerland*	10,523,964	72.58	4.3
Yugoslavia*	7,879,529	92.96	–8.7
Total	186,880,715	82.39	3.6

* = Arrivals of tourists from abroad in all accommodation establishments.
** = 1989
*** = Visitor departures at frontiers.
Source: World Tourism Organization 1992

more acceptable to the middle-class urban élite, who had looked down upon them as old-fashioned, rustic affairs. Yet these events formed part of the indigenous cultural legacy. This heritage became particularly important to a new nation searching for its cultural identity after imitating the drama and art of its foreign masters for more than 450 years. Thus, partly thanks to tourist interest, religious pageantry is beginning to play a new role in Malta. It is being accepted by government, many young intellectuals and, somewhat more grudgingly, by some members of the urban middle class as an important national asset. Increasingly it is figuring alongside sun and sea as part of the image that Malta projects of itself to qualify as an Other worth visiting. The general interest that tourists have shown in the country has increased Maltese self-confidence (Boissevain 1991).

There has been surprisingly little friction along the Mediterranean coast in summer between the mass tourist intent on celebrating sun and sea, and locals trying to do much of the same thing. Both are celebrating a brief period of freedom, a bit of anti-structure (a bit of the Other?) at the same time. But as the tourist gaze increasingly moves away from seaside ghettos in search of culture and unique events, it is reaching into backstage regions, gradually penetrating the daily lives and private domains of the hosts.

Cultural tourists, now growing bolder, are also setting out on their own to look at what has been sold to them. For example, in the Austrian village of Stuhlfelden, German tourists slipped uninvited into a private party and were observed peering into closed rooms and cupboards. The indignant hosts, keenly aware of the community's dependence on German visitors, were afraid to say anything (Droog 1991). In September 1993, Maltese friends celebrating the annual festa of St Leonard in Kirkop discovered two Germans peering about inside their house. The curious couple had come to the village with a festa tour, and had simply opened the glass inner door and walked into their brightly lit front room. Our friends politely showed them out. Then, to protect their privacy, they closed the wooden outer door that is always left open during the festa to display festive furnishings and decorations to passers-by.

Other anthropologists have recently reported the stumbling about of tourists in domestic back regions in Sardinia, Austria, the Lofoten Islands (Odermatt 1991; Puijk 1992). To protect themselves from such intrusion, but also to celebrate their own identity and re-create community sentiment eroded during the frenetic, competitive holiday season, host populations are closing certain attractions to tourists or celebrating when tourists are absent (cf. Boissevain 1991; Cruces and Diaz de Rada 1992; Crain 1992; Poppi 1992). Such episodes will multiply as cultural tourism is marketed to the masses. While intellectuals and guides in tourist destinations look forward to increasing cultural tourism, in the long run I think it will create more friction and have a greater impact on local culture than mass seaside tourism, where visitors were content to remain enclosed in ghettos.

Nostalgia

Another trend characteristic of today and likely to continue into the future is a romantic longing for an idealized past. Around the beginning of the 1970s a number of developments took place which affected attitudes towards the present and influenced thinking about the past. Established authority and the belief in continuing economic growth and its benefits were challenged, almost simultaneously, by the 1968 Paris student revolt; the anti-Vietnam War demonstrations in the United States; the sobering analysis of the Club of Rome's *The Limits of Growth: A Report on the Predicament of Mankind* (1972); the publication of Schumacher's *Small is Beautiful: A Study of Economics as if People Mattered* (1973); and, spectacularly, by the 1973 energy crisis and OPEC's challenge to the industrialized West. Seen collectively, these amounted to a serious reappraisal of just what the frenetic economic boom of the 1960s and the post-war drive for modernization had achieved. A concern for a new concept, the 'quality of life', emerged. This new look led to the reappraisal and idealization of, among other things, community customs and rituals and the 'traditional' community-centred rural way of life, abandoned in the quest for modernization. This reappraisal, in turn, has created an interest in the environment, history and traditional rituals, not to mention organic foods, working men's clothes, stripped pine furniture, home brewing, children's games, and farmhouse holidays. In Malta, for example, farming and craft implements, even ploughs and entire carts, have joined the classical statues, urns and swords that traditionally adorned the hallways and courtyards of the middle classes.

Nostalgia is being commoditized. The number of heritage parks and costumed pageants celebrating past events has multiplied spectacularly (Hewison 1987). For example, no less than £127.2 million was invested in heritage and museums in Britain during the first six months of 1988 (Urry 1990:105). Heritage and museums has become an industry. While until the early 1970s most British museums were publicly owned, 56 per cent of recently opened museums have been private ventures (ibid.:106).

The heritage industry purports to present history. But since 'traditional' artefacts are displayed and events are staged in part to mark boundaries and (re)establish community solidarity *vis-à-vis* growing numbers of outsiders, as well as to earn money, they invariably present an idealized, non-controversial, generally accepted version of the past. The past of most European communities was characterized by class conflict, exploitation, violence and factionalism. Authentic history, if displayed, would divide, not unite communities.

Sue Wright, for example, has described how in response to requests from local activists in a depressed district in north-eastern England, she and a colleague attempted to re-create community spirit by piecing together local history and symbols in a celebratory framework. Their efforts were only partly successful. Their invented galas were welcomed, but the authentic (critical) history that they had injected to stimulate reflection on the district's development problems was swiftly eliminated. Local residents and, in particular, politicians, found authentic history too politically divisive to be acceptable (Wright 1992).

Conclusions

Recent economic and political upheavals in eastern Europe and the steadily rising standard of living in western Europe have thus combined to increase ethnic and class heterogeneity, by bringing various categories of new Others – unemployed homeless locals, migrant labourers, political refugees, tourists – into established communities. This process will be accelerated as the Maastricht Treaty takes effect. The introduction of outsiders with widely different customs into relatively homogeneous neighbourhoods has created suspicion, jealousy and fear, and will continue to do so. Established natives have reacted by closing ranks, by attempting to re-establish contact with each other, by redefining and projecting the essence of their own identity through rituals, but also increasingly by means of violence. This action to establish clear boundaries between 'us' and 'them' is redefining existing communities and creating new communities. Everywhere in Europe 'communities' are multiplying and there is renewed concern with local identity and concomitant symbolic and physical activity at the interface between these multiplying communities.

While it is difficult to predict developments, it seems likely that the anthropology of Europe, at least for the next decade, will be influenced by the effects of the trends that I have attempted to set out. Thus, many of the next generation of anthropologists working in Europe will examine the emerging subcultures of the many new communities; they will explore the new modes of production; they will examine the nature of the escalating dialectic of racism and xenophobia that is engulfing Europe; they will examine the symbolic and political economic techniques communities use to confront each other and to mark and to protect their borders; they will try to understand the habits and motives of tourists and the reactions of the hosts; and they will further explore the nostalgia gripping 'post-industrial' society.

It is even more difficult to foresee the theoretical course such studies will take. What is certain is that there will be changes, if only because many in each generation seek to free themselves from the hegemony of the preceding generation (cf. Boissevain 1974). It is likely, therefore, that the present intense concern with symbolism, deconstruction and reflexivity will give some ground to a greater interest in the pragmatics of survival. When confronted with structural unemployment, growing homelessness, racist violence and neighbours who slaughter each other, a concern with speculative symbolic analysis and academic rhetorical techniques pales. Political and economic dimensions, recently somewhat neglected, may therefore become more important, as they were following the Second World War and decolonization. Their analysis can be enriched by insights developed during the past decade of intense cognitive and reflexive exploration. Perhaps this will occur with less concern for Self and more regard for Others. But I hold no crystal ball.

References

Bamford, J. (1987). The Development of Small Firms, the Traditional Family and Agrarian Patterns in Italy. In *Entrepreneurship in Europe. The Social Processes* (eds R. Goffee and R. Scase), pp. 12–24, London.

Bax, M. (1976). *Harpstrings and Confessions. Machine-Style Politics in the Irish Republic*, Assen/Amsterdam.

Blok, A. (1974). *The Mafia of a Sicilian Village, 1860–1960. A study of violent peasant entrepreneurs*, New York.

Boissevain, J. (1974). Towards a Sociology of Social Anthropology. *Theory and Society*, **1**, 211–30.

Boissevain, J. (1984). Small Entrepreneurs in Changing Europe. In *Ethnic communities in business. Strategies for economic survival* (eds R. Ward and R. Jenkins), pp. 20–38, Cambridge.

Boissevain, J. (1986). Residential Inversion: The Changing Use of Social Space in Malta, *Hyphen*, **5**, 55–71.

Boissevain, J. (1991). Ritual, Play and Identity: Changing Patterns of Celebration in Maltese Villages. *Journal of Mediterranean Studies*, **1**, 87–100.

Boissevain, J. (ed.) (1992). *Revitalizing European Rituals*, London.

Boissevain, J. and Friedl, J. (eds) (1975). *Beyond the Community: Social process in Europe*, The Hague.

Boissevain, J. and Grotenbreg, H. (1988). Culture, structure, and ethnic enterprise: the Surinamese of Amsterdam. In *Lost Illusions. Caribbean Minorities in Britain and the Netherlands* (eds M. Cross and H. Entzinger), pp. 221–49, London.

Bouquet, M. and Winter, M. (eds) (1987). *Who From Their Labours Rest? Conflict and practice in rural tourism*, Aldershot.

Brunt, L. (1974). *Stedelingen op het platteland. Een antropologisch onderzoek naar de verhouding tussen autochtonen en nieuwkomers in Stroomkerken* (Urbanites in the Countryside. An anthropological study of the relation between locals and newcomers in Stroomkerken), Meppel.

Brusco, S. (1982). The Emilian Model: productive decentralization and social integration. *Cambridge Journal of Economics*, **6**, 167–84.

Cohen, A. P. (ed.) (1982). *Belonging. Identity and Social Organization in British Rural Cultures*, Manchester.

Cohen, A. P. (1985). *The Symbolic Construction of Community*, Chichester, London.

Cohen, A. P. (ed.) (1986). *Symbolising Boundaries. Identity and*

Diversity in British Cultures, Manchester.
Crain, M. (1992). Pilgrims, *Yupeez* and Media-Men: The Transformation of an Andalusian *Romeria*. In *Revitalizing European Rituals* (ed. J. Boissevain), pp. 95–112, London.
Cross, M. and Entzinger, H. (eds) (1988). *Lost Illusions. Caribbean Minorities in Britain and the Netherlands*, London.
Cruces, F. and Diaz de Rada, A. (1992). Public Celebrations in a Spanish Valley. In *Revitalizing European Rituals* (ed. J. Boissevain), pp.62–79, London.
Droog, M. (1991). 'En Dan Word Je Weer Gewoon Mens.' Het opleven van feesten in een Oostenrijkse dorp (`And then you become human again.'The revival of celebrations in an Austrian village), unpublished MA dissertation, Department of Anthropology, University of Amsterdam.
Esmeyer, L. (1982). *Marginal Mediterraneans: Foreign settlers in Malta, their participation in society and their contribution to development*, Amsterdam.
Firth, R. (1954). Social Organization and Social Change. *Journal of the Royal Anthropological Institute*, **84**.
Gershuny, J. (1978). *After Industrial Society. The emerging self-service Economy*, London.
Gilligan, H. (1987). Visitors, Tourists and Outsiders in a Cornish Town. In *Who From Their Labours Rest? Conflict and practice in rural tourism* (eds M. Bouquet and M. Winter), pp.65–82, Aldershot.
Graburn, N. H. H. (1977). Tourism: The Sacred Journey. In *Hosts and Guests. The anthropology of tourism* (ed. V. Smith), pp. 17–31, Philadelphia.
Hewison, R. (1987). *The Heritage Industry*, London.
Ireland, M. (1987). Planning Policy and Holiday Homes in Cornwall. In *Who From Their Labours Rest? Conflict and practice in rural tourism* (eds M. Bouquet and M. Winter), pp.65–82, Aldershot.
Kuhn, T. S. (1970). *The Structure of Scientific Revolutions* (2nd edn), Chicago.
Leach, E. R. (1954). *Political Systems of Highland Burma*, London.
MacCannell, D. (1976). *The Tourist. A new theory of the leisure class*, New York.
Manning, F. E. (ed.) (1983). *The Celebration of Society: Perspectives on contemporary cultural performances*, Bowling Green.
Odermatt, P. (1991). Over de Nuraghen en Wat Verder Over de Zee Kwam. Een onderzoek naar het toerisme in Sardinië'

(Concerning Nuraghe and other things that came across the sea. A study of tourism in Sardinia), unpublished MA dissertation, Department of Anthropology, University of Amsterdam.

Poppi, C. (1992). Building differences. The political economy of tradition in the Ladin Carnival of the Val di Fassa. In *Revitalizing European Rituals* (ed. J. Boissevain), pp.113–36, London.

Puijk, R. (1992). Tourism and modernization in a Lofoten fishing village, paper presented at the 2nd Conference of the European Association of Social Anthropology, Prague, 28–31 August 1992

Sabel, C.F. (1982). *Work and Politics. The division of labor in industry*, Cambridge.

Schneider, J. and Schneider, P. (1976). *Culture and Political Economy in Western Sicily*, New York.

Turner, V. (1974). *Dramas, Fields, and Metaphors. Symbolic action in human society*, Ithaca and London.

Turner, V. (1983a). The Spirit of Celebration. In *The Celebration of Society: Perspectives on contemporary cultural performances* (ed. F. E. Manning), pp. 187–91, Bowling Green.

Turner, V. (1983b). 'Carnaval' in Rio: Dionysian drama in an industrializing society. In *The Celebration of Society: Perspectives on contemporary cultural performances* (ed. F. E. Manning), pp.103–24, Bowling Green.

Urry, J. (1990). *The Tourist Gaze. Leisure and travel in contemporary societies*, London.

Verrips, J. (1977). *En boven de polder de hemel. Een antropologische studie van een Nederlands dorp 1850–1971*, Amsterdam, 1977.

Verrips, J. (1980). The polder and the heavens above: An anthropological study of a Dutch village 1850–1971, *The Netherlands' Journal of Sociology*, **16**, 49–67.

Verster, A. (1985). Tweede Huis Toerisme in de Chianti' (Second house tourism in the Chianti), unpublished MA dissertation, Department of Anthropology, University of Amsterdam.

Ward, R. (1988). Caribbean business enterprise in Britain. In *Lost Illusions. Caribbean Minorities in Britain and the Netherlands* (eds M. Cross and H. Entzinger), pp. 204–20, London.

World Tourism Organization, (1992). *Yearbook of Tourism Statistics*, **2**.

Wright, S. (1992). Heritage or Critical History: The Re-Invention of Mining Festivals in North-East England. In *Revitalizing European Rituals* (ed. J. Boissevain), pp. 20–42, London.

Chapter 3

From the Mediterranean to Europe: Honour, Kinship and Gender

Victoria A. Goddard

This chapter addresses two areas of work that have contributed to the development of the anthropology of Europe. The first concerns the literature on honour and shame which was – and, for many, still is – central to the definition of the area of study. However, in this case, the area of study was not Europe but the Mediterranean. As was explained in the Introduction, the Mediterranean has been poorly delimited and theorized. Anthropologists have on the whole been reluctant to elaborate a clear definition of the area, and have instead followed a haphazard and contradictory approach, aimed at deriving a unity from the intrinsic characteristics of the data. Historians have been more successful here, and some anthropologists have taken their work as a point of departure for their own work, and as a validation of the area as an appropriate object of study (Braudel 1973; Davis 1977). Nevertheless, the general lack of rigour in defining the Mediterranean has undermined the potential contribution of workers in this area.

The first section of the chapter will examine some of the limitations of the Mediterranean literature on honour and shame in order to propose a broader comparative perspective than that offered by the concept of 'the Mediterranean'. The second section considers the study of kinship, which, as anthropologists inevitably point out, has been central to the discipline since the nineteenth century. However, studies of kinship in Europe raised a number of difficulties for anthropologists, not least because of the discipline's conceptual baggage and theoretical concerns, which were ill-suited to the analysis of European societies. Because of these difficulties, the study of kinship has focused largely on the family.

Although studies of the family were pioneered in urban research in Europe (e.g. Firth 1956; Firth, Hubert and Forge 1969; Bott 1957),[1] here too there was a significant shift away from studying within a European context and towards a Mediterranean one. Although here work on the family and kinship has had a lower profile than honour and shame, it has also been considered a central item on the research agenda. In a series of seminars held in Nicosia in 1970 to mark the birth of the new Mediterranean Centre, Peristiany identified the theme of Mediterranean family structures as one of the main foci of Mediterranean anthropological research because 'It provides an excellent tool for the investigation of "traditional" values and institutions and a useful introduction to the study of social change' (Peristiany 1976: 1). Yet general conclusions regarding the nature of kinship in European societies appear to break down the assumed `unity of the Mediterranean' cultivated by the honour and shame literature. It is this contradiction, latent within Mediterranean and European anthropology, which will be explored in this chapter.

Anthropological research in the Mediterranean has been largely concerned with small-scale communities and traditional cultural values. Assumptions regarding traditional society underscored work on both honour and kinship. Social change was generally seen as resulting from the impact of external modernizing forces which were either accommodated or resisted. While these assumptions provided an implicit basis for the continuity and legitimation of work in the Mediterranean, they have arguably limited the scope of inquiry.

Furthermore, within both these areas of research, gender ideals and gender roles constitute a significant, if not a central, consideration. In fact, the unity of the Mediterranean has often been predicated on the basis of the specific character of gender ideals that are purported to predominate here. This is the case with the earlier literature on honour and shame (Peristiany 1965; Campbell 1964) and is also stated more explicitly in some of the recent literature, particularly in the work of Gilmore (1987a). But although ideals of masculinity and femininity and related behaviour are

1. Firth's research in Britain was part of an innovative and ambitious collaborative arrangement with David Schneider, who carried out parallel research in the United States.

extensively documented and discussed, this is not done in the light of theories of gender. Rather, the material congeals around the pole of meaning of 'honour', generally understood to be male reputation, and gender difference remains assumed and untheorized. Gender issues are also prominent in discussions of kinship in the area. Peristiany (1976) argued that the different degrees and forms of integration of women into the different family types identified by anthropologists in the Mediterranean area provided important criteria for defining and characterizing these societies. The status of women has often been used as a gauge of the relative modernization and progress of individual societies and cultures (Goody 1983; Moors 1991). This, and the assumptions that inform this approach, have affected the development of the anthropology of Europe, and particularly that of the Mediterranean. Consequently, we find a paradox, whereby male and female positions and domains are exposed, yet remain untheorized in relation to gender.

It is from the perspective of gender that these two fields will be discussed, with a view to opening up exploration of more rigorous and more effective frameworks for comparison. The aim is to outline a critique of the category of the Mediterranean as an object of study. While Europe represents a more appropriate unit of analysis and comparison, we should be aware of some of the dangers involved in an uncritical acceptance of Europe as the alternative object of study. The paper suggests that gender provides a link between studies of kinship and studies of honour and shame, and that by integrating these fields progress can be made towards generating new proposals for anthropological research. These would enable us to suggest themes for research within Europe, whilst recognizing the value of comparisons on a wider basis.

Honour, Shame and the 'Mediterranean'

Peristiany's edited volume on honour and shame (1965) assumes that the Mediterranean is a relevant area of analysis, where patterns of behaviour allow for comparison and the drawing of general conclusions. These essays assert that in a wide-ranging area, from southern Portugal to Turkey and southern France to north Africa, people are preoccupied with reputation (apparently to a greater extent than elsewhere), and that this concern is embodied in concepts of honour and shame. The emphasis in the literature has been generally on honour – shame being seen as a rather residual category – and on male honour in particular. Later generations of anthropologists have raised many doubts and questions regarding these characterizations (Lever 1985; Llobera 1986; Goddard 1987; Herzfeld 1980; Pina-Cabral 1989) and many chose to circumvent these concepts altogether (Reiter 1975; Hirschon 1978), or to seek alternatives or modifications to improve a general framework (Herzfeld 1987; Giovannini 1987) or to take account of local specificities (Abu Zahra 1970, 1974; Wikan 1984; Loizos and Papataxiarchis 1991). Yet in spite of the problems raised, as late as 1987 the Mediterranean was re-proposed – or some might say confirmed – as a valid unit of analysis, which was to be defined, precisely, in terms of the honour and shame complex (Gilmore 1987b).

One of the consequences of a persistent anthropological focus on honour and shame has been a narrow restriction in the anthropologists' concerns. The reification of honour pre-empted the need for explanation and analysis. On the contrary, a number of institutions and practices have been attributed to the code of honour when they required an explanation in their own right. A second, and related problem, is that debates regarding the Mediterranean have taken place within an enclosed and self-contained discourse, and have effectively resisted the impact of inputs and developments originating in other areas of anthropological enquiry. Thus, although discussions regarding honour and shame revolve principally around gender relations and the construction of gender identities, there has been little exchange between the abundant material gathered under the auspices of honour and the impressive developments that have taken place in the study of gender within anthropology. It is significant that, with the exception of some of the early classical works on the Mediterranean, the by now bulky literature on honour and shame is noticeably absent from Moore's comprehensive introduction to the anthropological study of gender (Moore 1986). Another aspect of the self-contained nature of the honour theme is the inability of much anthropological work in the area to confront the global processes which impinge on local phenomena, a limitation compounded by the tendency to select rural or small-scale communities for the purposes of research.

Many anthropologists have felt uncomfortable with the

constraints and limitations of the dominant anthropological discourse on the Mediterranean. Giovannini, for one, has made a number of attempts to expand and refine the terms of the debate. Furthermore, her efforts have been guided by an awareness of gender difference as a social phenomenon rather than as an outcome of natural characteristics. Her suggestion that we focus on chastity as a circum-Mediterranean code represents an attempt to break with the limitations of the focus on honour (1987). In relation to her work in a Sicilian town she recognizes the impact of wider-ranging institutions, such as the State and the Church, and processes of socio-economic change, which she sees as playing an important role in conditioning cultural codes and behaviour (Giovannini 1981). She also emphasizes the importance of class and of the 'politics of gender'. However, her approach remains enclosed within the terms of definition of a Mediterranean culture area, and this inhibits the possibility of a fuller understanding of regional and national factors. In a later piece (1985), where she discussed the establishment of a small factory in a Sicilian village, Giovannini located the issues within a wider literature which went beyond the terms defined by Mediterranean anthropology and the honour code. This provided new opportunities for comparative analysis, linking State policies, entrepreneurial strategies and gender relations.

Giovannini argued that entrepreneurs in the area, already encouraged by State subsidies aimed at developing the South, were able to draw on local gender stereotypes to justify advantageous employment strategies. Furthermore, these stereotypes were an obstacle to the organizing capacity of women as workers. Giovannini links her own observations to the work of Nash (1985) and Safa (1980) to conclude that employment in industry did not bring about any automatic transformation in gender roles, or indeed in women's consciousness as workers and as women. On the contrary, she suggests that employment strategies may well reinforce pre-existing patterns of gender subordination.

What is significant here is that her discussion relates to a transnational enterprise, whose territorial mobility allows for investment patterns closely aligned with conditions which it deems to be favourable to its operation. Although several conditions are relevant (access to markets, to skilled labour for specialized operations, favourable terms regarding taxation, etc.), the pursuit of cheap and, preferably, passive labour is an important consideration. Women constitute a very high proportion of this cheap, malleable labour force. Indeed, similar conclusions to Giovannini's have been proposed elsewhere, not only in relation to factories in peripheral and semi-peripheral countries of Asia, Africa or Latin America but also in core areas, including areas of Europe. Harris' analysis of multinationals in Co. Mayo, Ireland, is particularly relevant here (1988).[2] As in the Sicilian case, factory production was established in Co. Mayo as a result of a combination of government incentives to industry and the opportunities offered by 'green labour', i.e., workers, in this case women, with little or no previous experience of wage labour and therefore little if any experience of unionization. Both Harris and Giovannini address the question of women's organization and militancy at work, but propose different explanations. Giovannini suggests that the capacity of women to organize is undermined by cultural symbolizations of women as 'virgins' or 'whores', which are ultimately divisive. Harris points out that the level of militancy of the Co. Mayo workers is determined by their own assessment of the conditions of existence of the firms which employ them. Given the unhappy memory of their mothers' and grandmothers' lives of struggle and hardship and their own negative experiences of making ends meet in the absence of locally available work, they are concerned to preserve their jobs, and therefore abstain from protest relating to issues which have a direct bearing on a firm's choice of location (for example comparatively relaxed legislation regarding health and safety). Yet the definition of gender roles is important here as well, not only in providing the specific commodity of (cheap) female labour but also in conditioning peer-group consensus. Thus, Harris explains the lack of enthusiasm regarding demands for child day-care facilities for women factory workers in terms of 'the ambiguities they themselves experience about the relation between maternity and paid employment and, also, from the social pressures imposed by their kin and friendship networks outside of work'(Harris 1988: 156).

Giovannini's approach, rooted in the idea of a Mediterranean cultural unity, ultimately confirms the view of traditional values

2. Although within a global framework Europe as a whole may be seen as a 'core' area, Europe is itself internally differentiated into 'core', 'periphery' and 'semi-periphery' (see Seers *et al.* 1979; Rokkan and Urwin 1983). It is significant that the examples discussed are provided by cases in peripheral, and heretofore rural, areas of Europe.

blocking progress. Harris, on the other hand, recognizes the importance of conceptualizations of gender roles, but locates these more effectively in their spatial and historical context. Nevertheless, both authors illustrate the fact that *women* workers have specific characteristics, not only in relation to their distribution in the labour-force, but also in connection with the factors that impinge on their attitudes and actions as workers. In fact, the significance of the cultural constraints affecting women workers is far from negligible. In the Sicilian town these arise from what Giovannini identifies as the elevation of 'woman' into a dominant symbol (Giovannini 1981). 'Woman' is conceptualized in positive terms as 'mother' and 'virgin', with the Virgin Mary as the paramount ideal. In opposition to these are the negative symbols of 'whore', 'witch' and 'stepmother'. But despite her efforts at elaborating a more comprehensive approach to the question of gender behaviour, Giovannini's horizon is still limited by the assumption of Mediterranean values, implicitly connected to the idea of 'traditional society'. Because of this she fails to contextualize these symbols adequately, and instead envisages them as pertaining to an autonomous symbolic level (associated with tradition) which may affect other areas of social life (for example, the process of modernization). Giovannini thus describes rather than explains, and what she describes are symbols operating within the field of traditional culture rather than within the domain of the 'politics of gender'. It would be more appropriate to consider the symbolic as an integral aspect of different practices. In the case of 'work', the symbolic can be seen as constituting not only the place and role of gendered subjects within specific tasks and industries, but the work-space and process of production and work itself (see Willis 1979; Hearn and Parkin 1987; Magaud and Sugita 1990).

By extending the comparative framework, the validity of Mediterranean values as an explanatory framework is undermined. If Mediterranean tradition cannot account for the ways in which women are conceptualized, the examples outlined might be read as suggesting that greater insights may be afforded by a consideration of the role of religion. This is a tempting alternative to an explanation based on Mediterranean values, given that, within a pseudo-evolutionary perspective, religious thought is often conflated with 'tradition', in opposition to secularization, rationalization and modernization. Furthermore, the view of the

Virgin Mary as ideal woman, and the symbolization of women which Giovannini describes, coincide with the symbolism and teachings of the Catholic Church. Both Ireland and Italy have a history of Church influence and intervention in national politics. In particular, the Roman Catholic Church has had a significant impact on State policy regarding family and sexuality, with important implications for women (Caldwell 1978). But this line of enquiry demands a careful analysis of the relationship between Church and State in each specific instance, rather than a reliance on 'traditional religiosity'. A historical dimension is crucial here, for, as Giovannini herself points out for the case of Italy, State legislation has altered significantly since the 1970s. In fact, there are strong indications that the Catholic Church has lost some of its power to influence government, and, more importantly, popular opinion, as illustrated by the defeat of the Church position in the referenda concerning both the divorce law and the abortion law in Italy in 1974 and 1981 respectively (Nanetti 1988).[3]

The importance of Catholicism (or religion in general) at both institutional and individual levels should not be underestimated. But Catholicism on its own cannot provide a satisfactory explanation for the behaviour of women in the labour market. Significant parallels are to be found in women's employment patterns and attitudes to work in settings which differ markedly in this respect. Pearson (1988) points out that the high concentration of women in the assembly phases of production in the UK electronics industry is comparable to figures from areas as diverse as the USA, Mexico and South-East Asia. The South Wales case studied by Pearson again shows parallels with the Irish and Sicilian material, in that multinationals were able to interact here with existing gender divisions. So here too the employment of 'green labour' facilitated the implementation of new forms of labour management, and discouraged unionization and militancy.

3. Changes in legislation are uneven and respond to very complex and often contradictory factors. Irish legislation is seen as less 'progressive' than that of Great Britain in some areas, such as abortion or divorce, whereas it is more 'progressive' in others. In 1993 Irish legislation equalized the age of consent for homosexual and heterosexual partners at 17. On 18 February 1994 the British Parliament voted against the equalization of the age of consent between heterosexuals and homosexuals at 16, and instead brought the age of consent for homosexuals down from 21 to 18. In this respect Britain lags behind many other European countries. There is also a perceived lag, publicized in the media, between the decisions taken by Parliament (e.g. *re* homosexual rights and hanging) and the opinion of voters. This is seen to raise issues of democracy and the role of government, which becomes particularly complex in relation to issues which are defined as pertaining to 'morality'.

Giovannini's questions regarding the weak militancy of the Sicilian women in her study can usefully be inserted in a wider framework. The implicit juxtaposition of Northern Europe and the Mediterranean, possibly inspired by the unstated contrast between a traditional Mediterranean and a modern North, has tended to reinforce the status of tradition (in this case the values of honour and shame or associated ideas) as explanation for a range of individual and institutional patterns. On the other hand, in this case, an explicit juxtaposition reveals important continuities. These support a critique of honour and shame as concepts with explanatory value, and force us to broaden, and deepen, our inquiry. Thus careful historical analysis, taking into account specificities of secular and religious institutions, provides an important backdrop to the analysis of gender and identity. We are then better placed to identify the specificities of local contexts. We can thus avert the risk of reifying into 'tradition' what in fact may be issues of power, domination and inequality.[4]

On the other side of the Mediterranean, parallel observations have been made with regard to Islam. The North African experience (and indeed, by historical legacy, that of part of Southern Europe as well) could be understood as deriving much of its character from Islam, its teachings and institutions. Such an explanation would be supported by assumptions regarding the opposition between traditional-religious versus modern-secular, and would furthermore reinforce certain assumptions regarding the opposition between Christianity and Islam, where the relative autonomy and oppression of women often plays a central role (Goody 1983).[5] But simplistic conclusions regarding both the impact of Islam and the relative status of women in Islamic cultures have been forcefully challenged. Wikan (1984) provides important insights in her data on Cairo and Oman by focusing on shame rather than honour, the latter being the discourse of official rhetoric and of arenas of male competition. Shame, on the other hand, is a point of reference in everyday life. By exploring shame, she shows

4. This is not to deny the significance of 'tradition'. In fact an appeal to 'tradition' can legitimize a practice or institution, or provide the basis for challenging them. But, echoing the structural-functionalists' discomfort with the evolutionists' use of 'survival' as an explanation of existing practices, I would argue that 'tradition' does not in itself provide the explanation for such practices, and the meaning and content of tradition must itself become the object of scrutiny.

5. Goody says: 'The Islamic world has often been looked upon as a purgatory for women, in implicit contrast to Christian Europe, a continent in which some see pre-industrial England as the particular paradise for the female sex (Macfarlane 1978)' (Goody 1983: 27).

that the system of values and their application is flexible, for the assessment of a woman by her peers is a complex matter, where sexual behaviour and indeed other behaviour is contextualized rather than judged in absolute terms. Local practices respond to a number of factors, and are more fluid and more 'autonomous' than the explanations in terms of 'honour' or Islam allow for.

Abu-Zahra (1970) argues that Islam itself varies historically and contextually (see also Al-Shahi 1987). She criticizes Antoun's explanation (1968) of the code of female modesty in terms of Quranic teachings, which he sees as having a constraining effect on women. Abu Zahra not only points out the sections of the Quran which claim equality for men and women (see also Tillion 1983; Goody 1983); but, more importantly, she warns of the very significant gaps which may exist between the erudite readings of the Quran by specialists and intellectuals on the one hand and popular views and practices on the other. There are wide variations in the interpretations of sacred texts and significant linguistic variations throughout North Africa and the Middle East which impinge on the meaning of the holy message. Furthermore, when we privilege Islam as an explanation of social and cultural phenomena, we risk neglecting the role of State policies and interventions. Abu Zahra points to the different national Personal Status Codes, whose contents vary from country to country. These official codes may not adhere to Islamic law, and may contradict the practices current in specific regions or villages, and thus provide a significant alternative framework or point of reference. What these criticisms suggest is that the relationship between dominant religious institutions, State institutions, and local practices is a complex and uneven one, thus making quite problematic the task of characterizing specific cultural areas.[6]

It is therefore misleading to focus on religion as the sole or primary cause of gender ideologies, without contextualizing the relationship between religion and the State and considering its contents and meanings in different localities and for different groups. But the links between State, religion and gender ideologies,

6. Another important consideration is the history of women's organizations and political movements. Moors (1991) suggests that the ommission of studies and/or discussions of feminism in Middle Eastern societies is a symptom of 'orientalism', where the status of women in Muslim societies takes on special significance. For an interesting discussion of the complex dialogues between feminism, Islam, and the West in Turkey see Sirman (1989). See also Kandiyoti (1989) for a discussion of the use of images of woman within State discourses.

flagged by a number of anthropologists, do remain an important consideration. For J. Schneider (1971) the weakness of the state in Southern Europe is identified as a central factor in the formation and centrality of codes of honour. Other anthropologists have argued that strong social concern with women's sexuality and roles reflects the production of boundaries and identities in response to specific State ideologies, as well as to commoditization and capitalist exploitation (Goddard 1987; Sant Cassia 1992). The exploration of the links between gender, family or household, State and religion, provides an interesting focus for comparative analysis, as illustrated by Asano-Tamanoi's comparison of Catalonia and Japan (Asano-Tamanoi 1987). She argues that whereas in Japan the State effectively incorporated men and women as household members, both within State ideologies and in connection with State-sponsored capitalist expansion, in Catalonia the household constitutes an impenetrable entity that beholds centralized authority with suspicion. What these works point to is the importance of integrating these different levels and fields – the local and the global, the personal and the public, the family and the State, which draws us away from a focus on traditional values as a dominant framework for the explanation of social behaviour.

In the early 1960s considerable effort was expended on the creation of an area of study which, though originally seen as integral to an anthropology of Europe, eventually established itself as a quasi-autonomous field of study (see Introduction): the Mediterranean. Central to defining the Mediterranean area was the question of values and their relation to gender difference. This resulted in the collection and discussion of a wealth of empirical data on men and women's behaviour, attitudes and outlook; but the data remained locked into the concept they were meant to define. Thus, an implicit or explicit reference to 'tradition', seen as opposed to the modernity characteristic of Northern Europe and the United States, restricted the field of enquiry and the depth of explanation of a number of institutions and practices. On the other hand, a focus on gender, problematizing gender difference, offers the opportunity of a broader – yet more focused – comparative framework. The explicit juxtaposition of North and South breaks down oversimplifications regarding the status of local tradition and of tradition versus modernity. From such a juxtaposition, it is clear that the problem of gender and work, for example, responds to more complex determinations. The perspective invites us to consider a number of different factors pertaining to the fields of the economic, the political and the ideological.

Gender and the Study of Kinship

While a focus on 'honour' led to generalizations regarding circum-Mediterranean culture, thus suggesting a unity between the southern areas of Christian Europe and Islamic North Africa and the Middle East, kinship studies often stressed the different histories and characteristics of the societies on the two sides of the Mediterranean (Goody 1983). The societies of North Africa shocked the anthropological world by their total disrespect for anthropological expectations. Here the preference was for lineage endogamy or 'keeping the girls of the family for the boys of the family' as Tillion (1983) put it. On the other hand, European societies were also seen to deviate from anthropological expertise and expectations, being characterized by a cognatic system. Anthropologists trained within the British tradition, so firmly anchored in African lineages, were frustrated in their efforts when working in the European context. Here they felt obliged to abandon the study of larger groups and to focus instead on the family and on marriage.

As in the case of honour and shame, a number of assumptions dictated the agenda for research that, coupled with the methodological difficulties already mentioned, discouraged the development of anthropological studies of kinship in Europe. The major influence here was the Parsonian view according to which societies evolved from a peasant social structure, where kinship was an important aspect of social organization, towards a modern society, where kinship lost most of its social functions and became exclusively the locus of sentiment, manifested in the expressive role of the family. Thus, from this perspective, kinship is seen to disappear in modern societies (Bestard 1986: 14, 20).

Strathern attributes this 'vanishing' to the Euro-American view of kinship, specifically the 'English' folk model, which she sees as informing anthropological theories. According to this model kinship is grounded in biology and is concerned with the 'basic facts of life'. As in the case of gender, the facts of kinship were seen to belong to the realm of nature, so that the anthropologist's role was limited to recording and explaining the variations found on a single, natural, theme (Strathern 1992a). Consanguinal relations were considered to be particularly close to the natural model and were seen as 'a virtual fact of nature, a universalism in human arrangements' (Strathern 1992a: 102). Cognatic kinship thus represented the background against which unilineal systems were constructed, and the cognatic systems of Europe appeared as a mere reflection of natural relations, seeming to offer the anthropologist very little potential for the construction of models (ibid.: 103).

Furthermore, in the post-Parsonian view, European kinship was considered to be qualitatively and quantitatively different from systems encountered elsewhere, for here, in contrast to primitive societies where family and kinship were clearly 'embedded', kinship belonged exclusively to the private, domestic sphere. This interpretation limited further the possibilities of exploring the conditions of production and reproduction of kinship and the reproductive strategies of wider groups, as well as the significance of kinship systems within contemporary European societies.

But in spite of these limitations developments did take place. In particular, Lévi-Strauss' distinction between elementary and complex systems of kinship and marriage offered the opportunity of locating contemporary European societies within the field of the comparative study of kinship systems. Héritier (1981) took up the challenge, and her work on semi-complex and complex systems helped place European kinship on a continuum with other systems, legitimizing and facilitating rigorous anthropological study. Her work, and that of others largely inspired by her, showed that over time there were significant patterns to the systems of marriage exchanges. The approaches that emerged from these insights were historical in orientation, and relied on a combination of oral accounts, family memory and official records and statistics, as well as the more conventional fieldwork methods (Segalen 1986; Segalen and Zonabend 1987; Zonabend 1984; Bestard 1986).

The importance of a historical approach becomes especially clear when we consider the tradition of research into the history of marriage, family and household in Europe (Flandrin 1979; Anderson 1980; Laslett and Wall 1972). A historical perspective also contributes to a clearer understanding of the central issues, and encourages the questioning of assumptions which underlie our approach to these phenomena, which is perhaps an especially important exercise in the European context (Rapp 1987).[7]

From the other side of the Channel, Goody challenged claims regarding the uniqueness of European kinship and society, implicit in the anthropologist's silence and explicit in much historical work, particularly that of MacFarlane (1978). Goody also espoused a historical approach to kinship; but rather than applying this to one region, he looked for systems in transformation over time and space (1983, 1991). He too is primarily concerned with marriage, but his focus is the transmission of property, specifically the impact of transmission of property to daughters. Here Goody stresses the influence of Church and State on local practices.[8]

But, as Segalen and Zonabend (1987) argue, there is more to kinship than the transmission of patrimony. It is also to do with the transmission of memory and the construction of identity. One of the most interesting developments within the field of studies of complex alliances in European settings is the understanding of kinship and marriage as constituent elements in the formation of identities, whether personal, local or regional (Zonabend 1984; Bestard 1986). Here again kinship links up with wider processes and institutions, reflected in the way family history evades, accommodates or transcends History – in the sense of events at the level of State and Church. At the same time, kinship is a central arena for the constitution of individual identities and for generating language, symbols and instruments for the construction of personal and more encompassing identities (Bestard 1986; O'Brien, this volume, chapter 9).

Kinship studies in Europe have demonstrated the significant variations over time and space that occur in the arrangement of relations between marriage partners, kin and affines. Although issues of property are frequently important considerations in these arrangements (and these have been studied in detail; see Friedl

7. For example, in Segalen's historical account of the peasant household in France (1983) the units of analysis – the household and the family – are problematized and therefore explored, as are gender relations. Indeed, this work contradicts many assumptions and simplifications regarding the peasant household, and indicates that there are significant regional variations in household form and patterns of exploitation of the land, as well as in the internal and external relationships which underpin them. Associated with these variations are different configurations of gender relations and different distributions of power within the household. Neither the household nor gender relations can be considered fixed and natural.

8. Both Christianity and Islam imposed conditions of limitation on local lineage groups, aimed at breaking down the autonomy and patrimony of such groups. Responses to these pressures ranged from lineage endogamy in North Africa (see also Tillion 1983) to a number of different patterns of endowment.

1963; Loizos 1975; Davis 1973, 1975; Du Boulay 1983; Sant Cassia 1992), the transmission and reproduction of 'symbolic capital' (Bourdieu 1977) is also significant, being central to the construction of identities. Wider-ranging identities, such as nationalism, borrow from the symbolic repertoire of kinship, and indeed of gender.

Because both gender and kinship are associated with the realm of nature, they are at one and the same time powerful sources of images and yet seriously under-theorized areas of study (Collier and Yanagisako 1987). This is particularly the case in the 'too-familiar' context of the study of European societies. The link between gender and kinship has been made explicitly and implicitly from a number of very dissimilar perspectives. For Collier and Yanagisako gender and kinship are constructed in a mutual relationship, and they are 'realized together in particular cultural, economic, and political systems'(1987: 7). This mutuality, though evident in so much of the literature, has not been fully recognized. Instead, the naturalization of both gender and kinship has pre-empted proper treatment and encouraged their conceptualization as two discrete fields, rather than as constituting a single field as envisaged by Collier and Yanagisako. As they suggest, 'both "gender" and "kinship" studies have been concerned with understanding the rights and duties that order relations between people defined by difference'. But difference has been understood as arising from natural rather than social facts (Yanagisako and Collier 1987: 29).[9]

In the anthropology of Europe, and of the Mediterranean in particular, the links between systems of kinship and marriage and gender identity have been recognized and discussed, though in many cases only minimally explored. However, as early as 1972, in his discussion of honour in Algeria and elsewhere in North Africa and the Middle East, Bourdieu explicitly linked the quality of honour to ideals of manliness. These ideals were in turn related to power, from which women were excluded except within the confines of an unofficial or even clandestine domain. Bourdieu's account of the kinship system is a gendered one to the extent that his analysis incorporated gender and power differences as an integral aspect of the system. He argued that many distortions in

9. Collier and Yanagisako recognize their indebtedness to D. Schneider's work on 'American Kinship', which criticized the biological model that he saw as pervading kinship studies. Instead, he promoted the study of kinship as a symbolic system. Collier and Yanagisako wish to suggest a parallel critique in relation to studies of gender (1987: 29).

the data resulted from the anthropologists' acceptance of the 'official' male version, neglecting the unofficial reading which comes from a female perspective. He suggested that men and women used and interpreted the same field of genealogical relationships in different ways. A consideration of both the 'official' and 'unofficial' versions revealed, for example, that the arrangement of marriages did not conform to a normative structure in any simple way, as many anthropological works imply. Instead, marriages depended 'on the state of the practical kinship relations', mobilized by men on the one hand and by women on the other. Thus, power relations, between groups and between women and men, determined the final outcome in each case.

Gender and Personhood

Howell and Melhuus (1993) argue that kinship studies lost their centrality within the discipline during the 1970s and 1980s and, especially towards the end of the 1980s, studies of personhood came to occupy the central arena. Here again gender was a central yet neglected consideration (1993: 7). Personhood and kinship, and the relationships that may hold between them, have been explored quite prominently in some ethnographic areas. Specifically, Strathern's discussion of the Melanesian Garia (1992a) is directly relevant, as this is a society which, like European societies, is cognatic. Nevertheless, the Garia conceptualize personhood in ways which differ radically from those current in Western cognatic societies, and the comparison encourages reflection on the characteristics of European systems and ideas, and the relation between the two.

Strathern suggests that for the Garia the person is composite and androgynous. The person is in fact constituted by and through relationships. This is the case not only for the cognatic Garia, but for other Melanesian societies as well, where the person is a cognatic entity, to be disassembled at death or in other life-crisis situations. The person is seen as embodying social relationships, which are integral to his/her being. There is thus a continuity between person and society which, she argues, is absent in Western European models. Here, the person is thought of as separate from or even opposed to society. Strathern suggests that the folk model of 'English' kinship sees kinship as incapable in itself of explaining social phenomena because of its incompleteness: the achievements of kinship have to be completed by 'society'. Similarly, the person is seen as an incomplete individual – completion has to be realized through socialization and through social relationships. Where kinship's socializing role ended, society took over. And in contrast with other systems, the cognatic system is seen to produce differentiation and heterogeneity. In English kinship unique individuals are produced as a hybrid, constituted by a specific combination of inherited genetic traits and completed by the experience of social relations.

Strathern's discussion of cognatic systems and personhood in Melanesian and Euro-American systems reveals not only the difficulties involved in comparative analyses, but also the complexities of the interrelations of kinship and person and conceptualizations of society and of the self. There is of course no simple correspondence between personhood and kinship type. Nevertheless, it is still useful to explore the ways in which kinship systems and family forms, residence patterns, or household relations are involved in the production and reproduction of personhood. Gender is an obvious consideration here, being an integral aspect of personhood in European societies.[10] According to Rapp, the Euro-American family 'is still the primary locus for the reproduction, transmission and transformation of cultural notions of gender and generation' (Rapp 1987: 125; also Barrett and McIntosh 1985). Rapp argues that this family type forms individuals with notions of gender which are tied to ideas of motherhood, and in particular with maternity, and of a fatherhood which is seen as revolving around economic responsibility. At the same time, `childhood' is imbued with ideas of progressive development.

This implies that the way the family is conceptualized and the way in which roles within it are constructed are generative of ideas of self and of relative power and exclusion that characterize the *different* selves that are created from this context (see Rubin 1975). The impact of ideals of motherhood on gender identity (especially but not only female identities) is, arguably, especially important in generating difference built on the basis of gender discontinuities.

10. However, as Strathern (1992a) points out, there is no one-to-one correspondence between gender identity and notions of personhood, and a particular individual may not have a singular gender identity. Howell and Melhuus (1993) also point out that more than one concept of personhood may exist in any given society.

For Irigaray, the symbolic universe expressed through family and kinship has particularly significant consequences for women's subjectivity. 'Motherhood' provides the focus for a definition of 'woman' which runs through the entire Western philosophical tradition. Whereas 'man' is recognized as separate and separable from 'father', there is no space within (male-centred) discourse for 'woman' disassociated from 'mother' (Irigaray 1977).

These considerations shed new light on Giovannini's Sicilian material. We are now further removed from Mediterraneanness and are closer to an understanding of these constructs of gender, and related symbols and images, as variants of a more pervasive discourse about social relations and conceptualizations of personhood and society (cf. Goddard 1988; Sant Cassia 1992). Furthermore, the difference created by this discourse is itself generative of differences in power, so that power is intrinsic to subjectivity and personhood.

There is a danger that, by concentrating on family and kinship, we may reproduce the conception of family and kinship as pertaining to an enclosed, private sphere, removed from, or even opposed to 'society'. This means not only that we reproduce ideological discourses regarding the family, but also that we limit and distort interpretation. For example, Loizos and Papataxiarchis (1991) express dissatisfaction with analyses of gender in Greece which over-emphasize the family as the domain for the definition and realization of gender relations. Instead, they propose the exploration of concepts of gender expressed beyond the family and outside marriage, where they may assume different forms, possibly challenging ideas of masculinity or femininity current in the language of kinship and family. Undoubtedly, there are many contexts where individuals and groups are able to shift and alter the conditions of their identity and sexuality, and these provide a useful focus of study. But the limitations they identify derive not so much from the anthropologists' overemphasis on kinship, as from a particular conceptualization of kinship: as distinct and opposed to the public arena or to the politico-jural domain (Collier and Yanagisako 1987).

It is more productive to see the family as 'an uncertain form whose intelligibility can only come from studying the system of relations it maintains with the sociopolitical level' (Donzelot 1980: xxv). From this perspective the family becomes a point of intersection of a number of often contradictory discourses and practices. For however the family might be thought about (as natural and permanent or as breaking down and in crisis) sociologically the family is seen as changing, as in a state of flux, as are the relationships that constitute it. In addition, this perspective obviates the dangers of studying the family as an isolated entity, to be understood exclusively in its own terms, abstracted from its historical context. On the contrary, there is an evident continuity between family and kinship relations and other relations that we can describe as social, economic or political.

The family has been at the heart of debates regarding social change, specifically the development of capitalism in areas of Europe, and indeed the successful development or otherwise of capitalism world-wide. The family has frequently been singled out not only as a relevant factor or indicator of social change, but also as a causal factor of this change and of the character of socio-political structures. The debates that have taken place in social history have largely revolved around the question of the specificities of the European or the English family and their consequences for the development of capitalism (Laslett and Wall 1972; MacFarlane 1978; but see also Anderson 1980; Goody 1983, 1991). However, the relationship between family form, individual orientations and social ideologies is hardly straightforward.[11]

This relationship has been explored by Todd (1985), who develops Le Play's classification of family types in Europe, concentrating on two central criteria, those of liberty and of equality, and their implementation within different family types. For Todd, the family reproduces people and values. The latter are absorbed unconsciously and automatically by each new generation from the preceding one, feeding into individual views and behaviour. Todd believes that the nature of what he calls the 'elementary' or 'human' relations that in each family type are produced between its members is then reflected in 'second' or 'social' relations. Thus, an egalitarian family structure will generate not only egalitarian sentiments between siblings but also a predisposition towards an egalitarian ideology in relation to politics and government.

11. Poster (1978) warns against the dangers of determinism, and argues that, in order to avoid a simple reduction of subject to family form, when studying the family we must incorporate a psychoanalytic dimension. In spite of the methodological difficulties, we should strive to understand the 'emotional structures' as well as the material implications of different family systems.

From Todd's perspective, 'the ideological system is everywhere the intellectual embodiment of family structure, a transposition into social relations of the fundamental values which govern elementary human relations...' (Todd 1985: 12). Just as MacFarlane explains the origins of English individualism and hence capitalism through the character of the English family, so Todd explains the French Revolution as an extension of values pertaining to the family type characteristic of the Paris region (1985: 14). He identifies two kinds of individualism: the liberal (but not egalitarian) Anglo-Saxon individualism generated by an absolute nuclear family type and the liberal and egalitarian 'Latin' individualism, associated with the egalitarian nuclear family type characteristic of many areas of France and Southern Europe as well as Latin America. These have different implications for the ideological and institutional characteristics of these societies. Whereas mass politics is now universal, Todd sees its form as depending on the orientations generated by different family types. Thus, he explains historical differences across Europe: National Socialism by Germany's authoritarian family, stressing discipline and inequality; Soviet Communism by the Russian community family, based on equality, discipline, parity between brothers and an authoritarian father-figure.

Strathern (1992b) also addresses issues pertaining to the relationship between family and society, between individuals and social structures, albeit with far greater caution. In relation to English kinship specifically, she stresses its characteristics of diversity and discontinuity. In the English system at least there is no simple reproduction and no direct continuity of form or type. Even ideas about change and continuity are discontinuous, since each generation embodies different ideas of change and tradition. Whereas the older generation come to stand for continuity and traditional values, the new generations are associated with change and a greater degree of individualism. 'Out of the fact and direction of generation, the antitheses between convention and choice or relationships and individuality acquire a temporal dimension.... Increased variation and differentiation invariably lie ahead, a fragmented future as compared with the communal past' (1992b: 21). Thus the way past, present and future are seen, and the way individual and society are conceptualized, is relational. Generational discontinuity might play a part in how we conceptualize history, and thus in the relationship between self and society.

Davis (1989) points to the usefulness of the generational dynamic discussed by Lisón-Tolosana in his work on Belmonte de los Caballeros. Here changes in context are significant. In Belmonte the 'controlling generation' had been adolescents and army recruits during the Spanish Civil War, and had thus experienced dramatic conflicts and dangers. Their experiences shaped their attitudes to politics, which were cautious. On the other hand, the emerging generation grew up in a quieter, repressive but apolitical world, and their attitude was more assertive, seeking greater freedom and independence. The relationship between the two generations was one of opposition. This oppositional relationship constituted the history of Belmonte between 1900 and 1961, a history of reactive response, of reinterpretation and discontinuities. Davis contrasts this generational form of history, which in Belmonte's controlling generation was a history of 'never again', with the genealogical and 'always so' view of history (belonging to the Zurwaya tribesmen of Libya) and the national (the Libyan State's) version of historical events which he encountered in his own research. These different histories reflect not only differences in context but also in the nature of the social relations (within families and generations, lineages, nations and states) which, as Davis points out, produce history.

'Being' is thus a product of context and of specific relationships. Generation and gender are powerful sources of difference as well as of symbols which speak of difference, discontinuity and inequality. Here again, content and meaning are contingent on the numerous relations and situations which produce them. Todd and others argue that different types of family or indeed of nuclear family involve different configurations of relations and patterns of power-distribution which have implications for gender relations. And if, as Irigaray suggests, motherhood represents the dominant theme in discourses of womanhood which generate and reproduce inequality, it would be important to explore the specific combinations of factors and relations effecting the elaboration of motherhood, and the extent to which and the ways in which these ideas might be deployed in other discourses.

Material and non-material factors combine to affect ideas of personhood. This is explored by Sant Cassia (1992) in his study of the family, and in particular of the transmission of property, in Athens in the late eighteenth and early nineteenth centuries. Sant Cassia shows how the ways in which exchanges of property and goods, together with values and morals, impinge on a number of domestic arrangements and on dominant ideals of motherhood and, more generally, parenthood. As a result of changes in the sphere of exchange, parenthood became central to ideas of personhood. Sant Cassia argues that in nineteenth-century Athens rapid commodification spilled over into the marriage circuit by commodifying dowries. The idea that women were themselves thereby becoming commodities was resisted through the growth and elaboration of a cult of motherhood, which was in turn reflected and expressed within the realm of religious doctrine. Marriage and parenthood became, in nineteenth century Athens, the principal channels for the definition and realization of the self. This was markedly different from earlier conceptions of personhood, which had relied heavily on genealogy and descent. The emphasis on parenting and especially on motherhood was also reflected in the growth of Greek nationalism, which used womanhood, and particularly motherhood, as metaphors for the nation.

The shifts that Sant Cassia traces at the level of the material exchanges in the economy and the marriage circuit represent significant points of change for conceptions of the person. To the process of commodification he introduces the concept of civil society, 'as a causative or shaping agent on the nature of exchange' (1990: 247). For Sant Cassia 'civil society' ultimately shapes the person, influencing and defining circuits of exchange, setting the context of the various spheres of action such as the public and the private, and the terms of exchanges, including marriage. The outcome is the co-existence of two types of morality in Greece: the competitive morality of the public – and male – arena and the morality of self-sacrifice associated with the family (ibid.: 250).

Civil Society and the Study of Kinship[12]

Gramsci (1973) outlined two superstructural 'levels' which he considered central to the understanding of society: 'civil society', 'the ensemble of organisms commonly called "private"' (p. 12), and

12. The concept of 'civil society' has a long trajectory in Western political discourse, and its content and meaning have varied significantly. For a useful overview of the use of this concept see Giner (1985) and Gamble (1981). For the purposes of this article my own use will be restricted to the work of A. Gramsci on this topic.

the State or 'political society'. The arena of 'political society' is to do with the State's use of coercion to enforce consensus; 'civil society' is the arena for the function of 'hegemony'. Both functions are for Gramsci 'organizational and connective'. Furthermore, the contents and the boundaries of civil society and political society shift historically, and are thus specific to time and place.

The connectiveness emphasized by the Gramscian perspective has been used to criticize current uses of the public/private dichotomy in the study of gender and to develop an appropriate model of the complexities and contradictions of women's activities in the realms of the family, the labour market and the state. Showstack Sassoon (1987) turns to Gramsci to move beyond the impasse reached by the 'domestic labour debate' and to avert the shortcomings of analyses which reduce the family to the needs of reproduction of capitalism. Showstack Sassoon points out that the relationship between women and the labour market is mediated in contemporary societies by the interventions of the State, which impinge on the family and on women's family labour. Thus, when analysing women, family and work, the intertwining of the domestic and the productive, civil society and the State becomes of central importance. The precise forms of institutions and of social relations are consequent upon the historical trajectory of each country, and of the groups that constitute it. This means that national variations can be considered while simultaneously recognizing common international trends and more general characteristics of late capitalism (Showstack Sassoon 1987:18).

A further advantage offered by the concepts of civil society and of hegemony is that they constitute a framework for seeing power relations outside the field of coercive state structures. This of course is especially relevant to the analysis of gender and kinship. More generally though, they provide space for the question as to 'how will each single individual succeed in incorporating himself into the collective man, and how will educative pressure be applied to single individuals so as to obtain their consent and their collaboration, turning necessity and coercion into "freedom"?' (Gramsci 1973: 242).

It has already been suggested that an approach such as that of Donzelot, which stresses the characteristics of the socio-political domain, is valuable for the study of family and kinship. Developing further the recognition that kinship is not an isolated field, the use of the concept of 'civil society' offers a basis for comparative work.

From this perspective the specific and the local can be understood within the context of changes taking place in a number of different sites. By locating kinship and family within civil society we are emphasizing the links between forms and relations within kinship and wider relations and processes.

It is increasingly clear that when looking at Europe, either historically or synchronically, we are dealing with multiple forms of domestic arrangements, marriages and inheritance patterns. Given the variety of arrangements, Balbo (1987) rejects the usefulness of the term 'family' and suggests that it be replaced by the concept of 'survival units'. Her observations regarding the inaccuracy of seeing 'the family' as nuclear and of this as constituting the norm are well taken. But as she points out, the term 'family' is a charged one. And it is precisely this which makes 'the family' or rather discourses about 'the family' interesting and important.

Balbo points to homosexual unions, single-parent units, couples living in communal arrangements, etc. Strathern's work too shows that there is complexity and differentiation, here seen as characteristic of English kinship. But this diversity does not pose an absolute obstacle to comparative work. The concept of civil society could provide the basis for such a comparative exercise by broadening the analysis out from kinship *strictu sensu* and including other sets of practices and ideas. Barrett and McIntosh's (1985) distinction between familial ideologies and family forms is relevant here, in that notwithstanding statistically significant differences at the level of family and household composition, familial ideologies (which may be somewhat more stable and pervasive than any particular morphology of the units themselves) are important in shaping a number of institutions at the level of the State and of civil society, as well as in providing points of reference and markers for individual experience and subjectivity.[13]

Europe as a useful (though not exclusive) framework for such comparison can be justified not only in terms of common or overlapping histories but also to the extent that the nations and states that constitute it share a number of ideals regarding the

13. Barrett and McIntosh distinguish between 'familism' and 'familization' on the one hand, and 'familialism' and 'familialization' on the other. The first two terms refer to politically pro-family ideas and to the strengthening of families themselves. The second pair of terms refer to ideologies modelled on what are thought to be family values and the rendering of other social phenomena like families (1985: 26).

nature of civil society, the role of the State and the forms and intentions of intervention, although the shape and extent of these vary significantly (see Comas d'Argemir, this volume, chapter 10). It is to be expected that increasing harmonization under the auspices of the European Community will result in greater convergence, not only in terms of ideals but, increasingly, in terms of institutions and policies. This is not to say that local practices will be homogenized or adhere strictly to these ideals. On the contrary, local interventions may vary and discourses and practices may take on specific meanings, even, possibly, meanings of resistance to such homogenization. Indeed the different incursions of the State into civil society, the changes in the shape of what it constitutes, may be resisted or accommodated in ways which further differentiate specific localities or particular groups. In fact, one of the expectations of greater European integration is that it will result in an enhancement of the us/them dichotomy, in relation to both external and internal others. It is precisely the tensions resulting from these contradictory processes, the transformations and the disjunctions between different discourses and practices, between civil society and the State, between these and practices and ideas in the fields of kinship, family and personhood which are of interest to the anthropologist, and where s/he can make a significant contribution.

Conclusion

There are precedents within European, and particularly in Mediterranean anthropology, for locating gender and personhood at the heart of family and kinship. The literature has often linked the study of family to ideals of personhood, largely as a result of the anthropologists' emphasis on personal reputation when working in this region. Pitt-Rivers for example suggests that a man's association with his family and his ability to defend it are the most important aspects of the group's assessment of his reputation (1965: 51). At the same time, honour is the central and connecting principle behind the contributions to Peristiany's collection on *Mediterranean Family Structures* (1976).

Peristiany identified family structures as a central area of Mediterranean research. Like Fortes and Evans-Pritchards' collection on African systems of kinship and marriage, Peristiany's collection is concerned with establishing a valid and coherent area of study. The essays included in the volume cover a wide geographical area and a broad range of themes. Indeed, the collection represents a number of different perspectives and problems, from the study of shepherds to the study of shanty-town dwellers. What the contributors illustrated was the variety of social arrangements, which could not be confined easily to any single formula or proposition. It is hard to see how any clear definition of an area, whether based on geographical criteria, on culture or religion could be accomplished, given the level of generality pursued and the empirical disjunction and lack of fit between the competing criteria for such a definition. The rich diversity of the contributions undermines Peristiany's implicit reference to cultural unity, and his task of bringing the various contributions together in his introduction is a difficult one. There is a tension here between the individual anthropologists, aware of the complexity of their case, and the efforts at generalization and at forging a unity which must have appeared as a necessary step towards academic legitimation. In fact, Peristiany has few general conclusions to offer, and his ultimate strategy is to provide a focus by looking at the relationships between women and kinship: the degree of integration of women in the different types of family and the impact of this on 'the intensity of their identification with their husbands' honour' (1976: 2) is, he suggests, a Mediterranean-wide problem, and also appears as the gauge of modernization and change. For Peristiany 'The relationship between degree of social integration, affective orientations and feminine conception of honour would well repay study in the Mediterranean area' (1976: 12). Thus, the question of honour, and indeed of gender, is once again the lens through which the unity of the Mediterranean is visualized.

Different kinship systems and different family forms can be expected to create different types of space for men and women, young and old, and to impinge on female and male subjectivities. More generally, these systems inform processes of acquisition of what Bourdieu calls 'the semi-learned grammars of practice' (1977: 20). Gender ideals and roles, generational relationships, ethnic and class relations, all these are apprehended through lived-in kinship. We should not take this to mean that there is a blanket correspondence between family forms and personality types or socio-political ideologies. As Strathern (1992b) points out, the

English kinship system produces individuals and it produces differentiation. In different ways and to a varying extent we can expect degrees of individuation, differentiation, change and heterogeneity elsewhere. But patterns are discernible. To begin with, heterosexuality is privileged, and marginalizes alternative sexualities and identities, as individuals and relationships are saturated with idioms derived from kinship. Such a privileging of heterosexuality coincides with the significance of parenthood and particularly motherhood as points of reference for the constitution of gender identities. Male and female ideals are intimately tied to ideas about performance in the field of kinship. Here the distinction suggested by Barrett and McIntosh (1985) is particularly useful, for whatever the arrangements of conviviality or commensality, of socialization and authority, familialism informs the processes whereby these differentiated individuals are developed, as well as providing discourses of community and nation with strong symbolic referents. Undoubtedly, beyond the idiom of kinship there are other sources of identity construction and other alternative, even contradictory, elements are available for the elaboration of other practices. Yet there is a continuity here between the person, kinship structures, civil society and the State, both in terms of how reproduction, sexuality and gender inform wider discourses such as nationalism and because there is no clear break in the continuum of actions and ideas, as has been suggested by the opposition between the public and the private or the politico-jural and the domestic domains.

The growing anthropological literature in the area, and in particular the heritage of work carried out in Southern Europe on gender and reputation, offers the possibility of developing that integrated field proposed by Collier and Yanagisako on the one hand and Howell and Melhuus on the other. The suggestion that gender can provide a bridge between until-now disparate areas of study is particularly suggestive. Howell and Melhuus' reference to the anthropology of the person is important. Although the category of the person frequently appears to be abstracted from gender, feminist philosophers and linguists have shown how this construct encompasses and subsumes women under what is essentially a male category.

Gender (at least in the European case, if the Mediterranean literature has any validity) is integral to the construction of subjectivities and to the organization of family and kinship. But the potential insights of perspectives which use gender as the pivot around which individuals and kinship structures might be analysed also have implications for wider identities and their mobilization in the political field. Thus not only can we further our understanding of gender and individual identity, but we are also led directly to the question of history and the changing shape of civil society. And it is here (and not in honour and shame, or a European family type) that we find the springboard for comparative analysis within Europe and between Europe and other areas. For it is in the historical evolution of the continuities and contradictions between ideas and practices of family, gender, individual and society that we can locate our understanding of different societies.

Both the studies derived from a Lévi-Straussian perspective and Goody's work on Eurasian systems go a long way in breaking down assumptions about the discontinuities between Europe and others, and the consequent discontinuities between the anthropology of European societies and the discipline as it has developed elsewhere. Recent studies have accentuated these insights, and the parallels and differences between, for example, English and Melanesian kinship have become clearer and have offered fresh insights. The work of anthropologists in the field of kinship studies in Europe has therefore been extremely productive, and the anthropologist is now well placed to develop a fruitful field. However, taking our cue from Goody, we should bear in mind that Europe as a valid focus or unit of study must be problematized and assumptions of uniqueness avoided, for they have in fact thwarted the anthropological effort here, segregating the discussion and parochializing the terms of reference.

Tillion characterized Mediterranean societies in terms of 'the republic of cousins' (1983). This she contrasted to the 'republic of brothers-in-law' which she saw as characteristic of 'so-called savage society' and the 'republic of citizens' for those societies located in 'the modern sector' (1983: 13). Another way of discussing the qualitative differences between these types could be in terms of the nature of the relations which govern civil society and the relation between civil society and the State. The history and the nature of the interconnections between State, civil society and religion in European and North African countries show significant differences, as well as obvious parallels. A pressing question is that of the relative secularization of the State and of civil society. Given that sexual behaviour, gender roles and women's status are an important focus for secular and religious discourses and interventions, the study of gender and kinship must take into account the contradictory messages and processes unleashed by the relation between State and civil society.

Mediterranean anthropology explored some of the issues relating to the links and gaps between locality and national state, although these attempts have been limited by an emphasis on networks, particularly in the literature on patron–client relations. Ineffectual state bureaucracies have frequently been put forward as causal to certain characteristics of the Mediterranean, from patronage and *mafia* to the code of honour. Anthropologists have been well placed to examine the tensions which may exist between state structures and local relations and between national and local ideologies (Silverman 1975; Pratt 1980; Davis 1989), a tension which can produce 'good patriots' but 'rebellious citizens' (Herzfeld 1985: 26). This of course is an important issue when considering how civil society is constituted and how individuals and groups may or may not respond to or be incorporated into civil society. The question of national and local histories is important here both in terms of how state ideologies might attempt to encompass groups (Davis 1989) and how localities construct a 'social memory' which defines the boundaries and character of localities and their relation to the State as well as to history (Collard 1989; SEGRG 1992; also Zonabend 1984).

The comparison of Northern and Southern shores of the Mediterranean, pioneered by Mediterranean anthropologists, is both feasible and fruitful, given historical convergence and differences. This is not only so in the fields of kinship and gender, but applies also to national identity and the nature of civil society (cf. Davis 1987). The comparison is the more fruitful if it escapes the constraints of the anthropological focus on the honour code. Thus, groups or individual men and women can be located in their practices and relationships (where discourses of honour or tradition may or may not play a part), while these are understood as aspects of wider processes. A systematic comparison which takes account of specific histories, concrete forms and relations between State, religion and civil society, would avoid reproducing the assumptions underlying 'the Mediterranean'. In relation to gender, the continuities and differences revealed by a comparison of European and North African cases can only enrich our understanding; but this must be accomplished on the basis of rigorous and clearly defined terms of comparison, and not within the complacent climate generated by a reliance on Mediterranean values and tradition.

A similarly productive, and urgent, exercise would be a comparison between Western and Eastern Europe. Gramsci argued that, at the time of his writing, in most advanced countries civil society had become a very complex structure. The history of these countries could be summarized as one of increasing secularization of the State and civil society. On the other hand, speaking for Russia up to the Second World War, Gramsci described a situation in which 'the State was everything, civil society was primordial and gelatinous' (1973: 238). The very specific transformation of State and civil society in Russia or elsewhere in Eastern Europe since that period and the rapid and dramatic changes that have affected the ex-Comecon countries make for very particular configurations of relations and ideas in connection with the State and civil society, with important implications for gender and kinship relations and ideologies.

The argument of this chapter is that we have much to glean from Mediterranean anthropology. The way forward, however, is not to reproduce the terms and concepts of that specialization but instead to broaden the analysis in two senses. One is that gender and kinship should be understood as relevant to personhood, while located within the broader contexts of civil society and indeed in connection with the construction of far-reaching identities such as nationalism. Secondly, that Europe rather than the Mediterranean should constitute the central scope of comparative analysis, although this should not be a restrictive focus. Indeed, there is much to be gained by placing European societies within a wider context of study, just as recent anthropologists have placed European kinship and marriage on a continuum with other systems, bringing Europe into the anthropological universe.

References

Abu Zahra, N. (1970). On the Modesty of Women in Arab Muslim Villages. A Reply. *American Anthropologist*, **72**, 1079–88.

Abu Zahra, N. (1974). Material Power, Honour, Friendship and the Etiquette of Visiting. *Anthropological Quarterly*, **47**, (1), 120–38.

Al-Shahi, A. (ed.) (1987). *The Diversity of the Muslim Community. Anthropological Essays in Memory of Peter Lienhardt*, London: Ithaca.

Anderson, M. (1980). *Approaches to the History of the Western Family. 1500–1914*. London: Macmillan.

Antoun, R. (1968). On the Modesty of Women in Arab Muslim Villages: a Study in the Accommodation of Tradition. *American Anthropologist*, **70**, 671–97.

Asano-Tamanoi, M. (1987). Shame, Family, and State in Catalonia and Japan. In *Honor and Shame and the Unity of the Mediterranean* (ed. D. Gilmore), Washington: American Anthropological Association Special Publication No. 22.

Balbo, L. (1987). Crazy quilts: rethinking the welfare state debate from a woman's point of view. In *Women and the State* (ed. A. Showstack Sassoon), London: Routledge.

Barrett, M. and McIntosh, M. (1985). *The Anti-Social Family*, London: Verso.

Bestard, J. C. (1986). *Casa y Familia. Parentesco y reproducción domestica en Formentera*, Palma de Mallorca: Institut D'Estudis Balearics. English transl. 1991 *What's in a Relative? Household and Family in Formentera*, Oxford: Berg.

Bott, E. (1957). *Family and Social Networks*, London: Tavistock.

Bourdieu, P. (1977). *Outline of a Theory of Practice*, Cambridge: Cambridge University Press. First published 1972 in Switzerland: Librairie Droz.

Braudel, F. (1973). *The Mediterranean and the Mediterranean World in the Age of Philip II*, London: Collins.

Caldwell, L. (1978). Church, State and Family: the Women's Movement in Italy. In *Feminism and Materialism. Women and Modes of Production* (eds A. Kuhn and A. M. Wolpe), London: RKP.

Campbell, J. K. (1964). *Honour, Family and Patronage. A Study of Institutions and Moral Values in a Greek Mountain Community*, Oxford: Clarendon Press.

Collard, A. (1989). Investigating 'social memory' in a Greek context. In *History and Ethnicity* (eds E. Tonkin, M. McDonald and M. Chapman), London/NY: Routledge.

Collier, J. F. and Yanagisako, S. J. (1987). Introduction to *Gender and Kinship. Essays toward a Unified Analysis* (eds J. F. Collier and S. J. Yanagisako), Stanford, California: Stanford University Press.

Davis, J. (1973). *Land and Family in Pisticci*, London: Athlone Press.

Davis, J. (1975). An Account of Changes in the Rules of Transmission of Property in Pisticci 1814–1961. In *Mediterranean Family Structures* (ed. J. G. Peristiany), Cambridge: Camridge University Press.

Davis, J. (1977). *Peoples of the Mediterranean. An Essay in Comparative Social Anthropology*, London: RKP.

Davis, J. (1987). Family and State in the Mediterranean. In *Honor and Shame and the Unity of the Mediterranean* (ed. D. Gilmore), Washington: Special Publication of the American Anthropological Association No. 22, 22–34.

Davis, J. (1989). The Social Relations of the Production of History. In *History and Ethnicity* (eds E. Tonkin, M. McDonald and M. Chapman), ASA Monograph 27, London: Routledge.

Donzelot, J. (1980). *The Policing of Families. Welfare versus State*, London: Macmillan. Original publication 1977 Les Editions de Minuit.

Du Boulay, J. (1983). The Meaning of Dowry Changing Values in Rural Greece. *Journal of Modern Greek Studies*, **1**, (1), 243–70.

Firth, R. (ed.) (1956). *Two Studies of Kinship in London*, LSE Monographs in Social Anthropology No. 15.

Firth, R., Hubert, J. and Forge, A. (1969). *Families and their Relatives. Kinship in a Middle-Class Sector of London*, London: RKP.

Flandrin, J. L. (1979). *Families in Former Times*, Cambridge: CUP.

Friedl, E. (1963). Some Aspects of Dowry and Inheritance in Boeotia. In *Mediterranean Countrymen: Essays in the Social Anthropology of the Mediterranean* (ed. J. Pitt-Rivers), Paris: Mouton.

Gamble, A. (1981). *Introduction to Modern Social and Political Thought*, London: Macmillan.

Gilmore, D. (1987a). The Shame of Dishonor. *Honor and Shame and the Unity of the Mediterranean* (ed. D. Gilmore), Washington: Special Publication of the American Anthropological Association No. 22: 2–21.

Gilmore, D. (ed.) (1987b). *Honor and Shame and the Unity of the Mediterranean*, Washington: Special Publication of the American Anthropological Association No. 22.

Giner, S. (1985). *Comunió, domini, innovació*, Barcelona: Laia.

Giovannini, M. (1981). Woman: A Dominant Symbol within the Cultural System of a Sicilian Town. *Man*, **16**, 408–26.

Giovannini, M. (1985). The Dialectics of Women's Factory Work in a Sicilian Town. *Anthropology*, **9**, (1/2), 45–64.

Giovannini, M. (1987). Female Chastity Codes in the Circum-Mediterranean: Comparative Perspectives. In *Honor and Shame and the Unity of the Mediterranean* (ed. D. Gilmore), Washington DC: Special Publication of the American Anthropological Association No. 22. pp 61–74

Goddard, V. (1987). Honour and Shame: the Control of Women's Sexuality and Group Identity in Naples. In *The Cultural Construction of Sexuality* (ed. P. Caplan), London: Tavistock.

Goddard, V. (1988). *Women and Work: the case of Neapolitan outworkers*, Unpublished Ph.D thesis, University of London.

Goody, J. (1983). *The Development of the Family and Marriage in Europe*, Cambridge: CUP.

Goody, J. (1991). *The Oriental, The Ancient and the Primitive. Systems of Marriage and the Family in Pre-Industrial Societies of Eurasia*, Cambridge: CUP.

Gramsci, A. (1973). *The Prison Notebooks*, London: Lawrence & Wishart.

Harris, L. (1988). Women's Response to Multinationals in County Mayo. In *Women and Multinationals in Europe* (eds D. Elson and R. Pearson), London: Macmillan.

Hearn, J. and Parkin, W. (1987). *'Sex at Work'. The Power and Paradox of Organization Sexuality*, Brighton: Wheatsheaf.

Héritier, F. (1981). *L'Exercise de la Parenté*, Paris: Editions du Seuil.

Herzfeld, M. (1980). Honor and Shame: Problems in the Comparative Analysis of Moral Systems. *Man*, **16**, 339–51.

Herzfeld, M. (1985). *The Poetics of Manhood. Contest and Identity in a Cretan Mountain Village*, Princeton: Princeton University Press.

Herzfeld, M. (1987). 'As in your own house': Hospitality, Ethnography, and the Stereotype of Mediterranean Society. In *Honor and Shame and the Unity of the Mediterranean* (ed. D. Gilmore), Washington: Special Publication of the American Anthropological Association No. 22. 75–89.

Hirschon, R. (1978). Open Body/Closed Space: the Transformation of Female Sexuality. In *Defining Females* (ed. S. Ardener), London: Croom Helm.

Howell, S. and Melhuus, M. (1993). The Study of Kinship, the Study of the Person; a study of gender? In *Gendered Anthropology* (ed. T. Del Valle), London, New York: Routledge.

Irigaray, L. (1977). *Ce Sexe qui n'en est pas un*, Paris: Editions de Minuit.

Kandiyoti, D. (1989). Women and the Turkish State: Political Actors or Symbolic Pawns? In *Woman-Nation-State* (eds N. Yuval-Davis and J. F. Anthias), London: Macmillan.

Laslett, P. and Wall, R. (1972). *Household and Family in Past Time*, Cambridge: Cambridge University Press.

Lever, A. (1985). Honour as Red Herring. *Critique of Anthropology*, **6**, (3), 83–106.

Llobera, J. R. (1986). Fieldwork in Southwestern Europe. *Critique of Anthropology*, **6**, (2), 333–49.

Loizos, P. (1975). Changes in Property Transfers among Greek Cypriot Villages. *Man*, **10**, 502–23.

Loizos, P. and Papataxiarchis, E. (eds) (1991). *Contested Identities. Gender and Kinship in Modern Greece*, Princeton: Princeton University Press.

MacFarlane, A. (1978). *The Origins of English Individualism. The Family, Property and Social Transition*, Oxford: Blackwell.

Magaud, J. and Sugita, K. (1990). *A Propos d'une comparaison franco-japonaise: le retour des réseaux.* Paper presented to the Séminaire franco-brésilien: Autours du 'modèle' Japonais.

Moore, H. (1986). *Feminism and Anthropology*, Oxford: Polity Press.

Moors. A, (1991). Women and the Orient: A Note on Difference. In *Constructing Knowledge. Authority and Critique in Social Science* (eds L. Nencel and P. Pels), London: Sage.

Nanetti, R. (1988). *Growth and Territorial Policies: the Italian Model of Social Capitalism*, London/New York: Pinter Publishers.

Nash, J. (1985). Segmentation of the Work Process in the International Division of Labour. *Contemporary Marxism*, **2**, 25–45.

Pearson, R. (1988). Women's Employment and Multinationals in the UK: Restructuring and Flexibility. In *Women's Employment and Multinationals in Europe* (eds D. Elson and R. Pearson), London: Macmillan Press.

Peristiany, J. (ed.) (1965). *Honour and Shame. The Values of Mediterranean Society*, London: Weidenfeld & Nicolson.

Peristiany, J. (ed.) (1976). *Mediterranean Family Structures*, published in association with the Social Research Centre, Cyprus, Cambridge: CUP.

Pina-Cabral, J. (1989). The Mediterranean as a Category of Regional Comparison: A Critical View. *Current Anthropology*, **30**, (3), 399–406.

Pitt-Rivers, J. (1965). Honour and Social Status. In *Honour and Shame. The Values of Mediterranean Society* (ed. J. D. Peristiany),

Chicago/London: Chicago University Press.

Poster, M. (1978). *Critical Theory of the Family*, London: Pluto Press.

Pratt, G. (1980). A Sense of Place. In *'Nation' and 'State' in Europe: Anthropological Perspectives* (ed. R. Grillo), London: Academic Press.

Rapp, R. (1987). Toward a Nuclear Freeze? The Gender Politics of Euro-American Kinship Analysis. In *Gender and Kinship. Essays toward a Unified Analysis* (eds J. F. Collier and S. J. Yanagisako), Stanford: SUP.

Reiter, R. (1975). Men and Women in the South of France: Public and Private Domains. In *Toward an Anthropology of Women* (ed. R. Reiter), New York: Monthly Review Press.

Rokkan, S. and Urwin, D. (1983). *Economy, Territory, Identity. Politics of Western European Peripheries*, London: Sage.

Rubin, G. (1975). The Traffic in Women: Notes on the 'Political Economy' of Sex. In *Toward an Anthropology of Women* (ed. R. Reiter), New York: Monthly Review Press.

Safa, H. (1980). Class Consciousness among Working-class Women in Latin America: Puerto Rico. In *Sex and Class in Latin America* (eds J. Nash and H. Safa), New York: Bergin Press.

Sant Cassia, P. (with C. Bada) (1992). *The Making of the Modern Greek Family. Marriage and Exchange in 19th Century Athens*, Cambridge: Cambridge University Press.

Schneider, D. and Homans, G. (1955). Kinship Terminology and the American Kinship System. *American Anthropologist*, **57**, 194–208.

Schneider, J. (1971). Of Vigilance and Virgins: Honor, Shame and Access to Resources in Mediterranean Societies. *Ethnology*, **10**, 1–24.

Seers, D., Schaeffler, B. and Kiljunen, M. L. (eds) (1979) *Underdeveloped Europe*, London: Harvester Press.

Segalen, M. (1983). *Love and Power in the Peasant Family. Rural France in the 19th Century*, Oxford: Blackwell.

Segalen, M. (1986). *An Anthropological History of the Family*, Cambridge: Cambridge University Press.

Segalen, M. and Zonabend, F. (1987). Social Anthropology and the Ethnology of France: The field of kinship and the family. In *Anthropology at Home* (ed. A. Jackson), ASA monograph 25, London: Tavistock.

SEGRG (1992). The relevance of Gender for the Anthropology of Europe: Gender and the Politics of Difference. Conference on 'The Anthropology of Europe: 1992 and After', London:

Goldsmiths College.

Showstack Sassoon, A. (1987). Introduction: the Personal and the Intellectual, Fragments and Order, International Trends and National Specificities. In *Women and the State* (ed. A. Showstack Sassoon), London: Routledge.

Silverman, S. (1975). *Three Bells of Civilization: the Life of an Italian Hill Town*, NY: Columbia University Press.

Sirman, N. (1989). Feminism in Turkey: A Short History. *New Perspectives on Turkey*, **3**, (1), 1–34.

Strathern, M. (1992a). *Reproducing the Future*, Manchester: Manchester University Press.

Strathern, M. (1992b). *After Nature: English Kinship in the Late 20th Century*, Cambridge: Cambridge University Press.

Tillion, G. (1983) [1966]. *The Republic of Cousins. Women's Oppression in Mediterranean Society*, London: Al Saqi Books. Original publication *Le Harem et les Cousins*, Paris: Editions du Seuil.

Todd, E. (1985). *The Explanation of Ideology. Family Structures and Social Systems*, Oxford: Blackwell. Original publ. *La Troisième Planète, structures familiales et Systèmes Idéologiques*, Paris: Editions du Seuil.

Wikan, U. (1984). Shame and Honour: a Contestable Pair. *Man*, **29**, 635–52.

Willis, R, (1979). Shop Floor Culture, Masculinity and the Wage-Form. In *Working Class Culture* (eds J. Clarke, C. Critches and R. Johnson), London: Hutchinson.

Yanagisako, S. J. and Collier, J. F. (1987). Toward a Unified Analysis of Gender and Kinship. In *Gender and Kinship. Essays toward a Unified Analysis* (eds J. F Collier and S. J. Yanagisako), Stanford, California: Stanford University Press.

Yuval-Davis, N. and Anthias, F. (eds) (1989). *Woman-Nation-State*, Basingstoke: Macmillan.

Zonabend, F. (1984). *The Enduring Memory. Time and History in a French Village*, Manchester: Manchester University Press.

Chapter 4

Anthropological Approaches to the Study of Nationalism in Europe. The Work of Van Gennep and Mauss

Josep R. Llobera

Introduction

The neophyte anthropologist who is interested in studying the national question in Europe will inevitably experience a sense of despair when he/she discovers the meagre theoretical legacy left by our classical ancestors in this area of knowledge (even when the word anthropological ancestor is understood in a generous manner). It is true that Durkheim and the Durkheimian tradition offer more possibilities than are usually acknowledged. I have myself explored in some detail Durkheim's contribution to the study of the national question (Llobera 1994). In addition, the work of Maurice Halbwachs (1980, 1992) in the area of the *mémoire collective* has obvious implications for the study of the nation; after all, the nation has strong, though complex, historical roots, and any attempt to unravel the symbolic and emotive use of the past can throw light on its nature.

An author who seems to have been totally ignored in all the anthropological attempts to recover what the past of the discipline has to offer on the study of nationalism is Arnold van Gennep. The main purpose of this paper is to present van Gennep's contribution to the study of the national question; I will also examine in some detail Mauss's inquiry on the nation. No doubt the important event which exercised the mind of these two leading anthropologists in this direction was the partial application of the principle of self-determination after the First World War to the constituent parts of the Austro-Hungarian and Ottoman empires. The fact that both contributions remained unfinished and fragmentary (particularly that of Mauss) may be the result of the appearance of more pressing anthropological pursuits – as Henri Lévy-Bruhl (1953–4) suggests for Marcel Mauss – or simply that the task was more difficult and complex than they had anticipated.

In van Gennep's case the contribution is substantial: it consists of a book and four articles. The book, the first volume of a *Traité comparatif des Nationalités*, was entitled *Les éléments exterieurs de la Nationalité*, and was published in 1922 (1922a); two other promised volumes – *La Formation de la Nationalité* and *La Vie des Nationalités* – were never published. The articles were published between 1920 and 1922. They relate nationality to a variety of factors: class (1921a), land (1921b) and religion (1922b); there is also a study of the formation and maintenance of Georgian nationality (1920). Why van Gennep's contribution should have been silenced or not recognized by the anthropological community is not an issue that is easy to explain. He suffered the fate of many other French social scientists who were eclipsed by the Durkheimian School.

Marcel Mauss's contribution is centred around 50 pages of text comprising fragmentary notes on a treatise of *La Nation* (1969a); the writings date from 1920 or 1921 and were published in *L'Année Sociologique* in 1953–4. Mauss published a short paper on 'La Nation et l'internationalisme' in 1920 (Mauss 1969b).

Arnold van Gennep

Van Gennep's book presents itself as a scientific study of the nationality (*nationalité*) based on a comparative study of a large number of empirical cases – which he labels the 'ethnographic method'. The geographic horizon is essentially European, and the study uses not only published material but also fieldnotes collected by the author over a four-year research period in southern Poland, while travelling in different parts of Europe, and on two scientific expeditions to North Africa (p. 9). What is at stake for van Gennep is to map out the different factors that give rise to what he calls 'nationalitarian forces' (*forces nationalitaires*); this process, which started in Western Europe, spread elsewhere as soon as the conditions for the appearance of national sentiments were in place (p. 10).

Nationalities are taken to be normal social phenomena, even if the author may deplore the fact that nationalitarian sentiments are sometimes used to justify conflict, violence, war, and massacres. What interests van Gennep are the strong notions and sentiments associated with nationalities, particularly when they are oppressed by an alien state. To ignore the role of nationalities at the level of world politics is the same as pretending that strong passions do not exist (p. 11). Nationalitarian sentiments are extremely powerful, and often take precedence over economic arguments (p. 12).

I have already indicated that van Gennep takes nationalities as given, and to a certain extent he also accepts as part of social life nationality struggles – even if he hopes to contribute transactional and negotiated solutions to the violent confrontations among nationalities. In other words, for van Gennep nationalities are here to stay, even if he does not enter into the question of whether they have a natural right to exist. This 'special political phenomenon is the result of a combination of ideas, sentiments and wills' (p. 12); it is a dynamic phenomenon, a 'tendential movement', and hence essentially unstable, which is affected by a variety of forces, some of which promote cohesion, others which encourage dissociation (p. 13). In the final instance, what matters is is to be able to map out the main features that distinguish nationalities from other systems of mass grouping' (ibid.).

Van Gennep's decision to focus on 'nationalities' rather than 'nations' is not without theoretical consequences. The term 'nationality', as it was used in France and elsewhere in the nineteenth and early twentieth centuries, indicated the will to exist as a nation of a group of people united by a community of territory, language, culture, history, etc. Closely connected, but independent, was the principle of nationalities, which asserted the right of these groups to constitute themselves in politically independent states. Van Gennep was well aware that it was difficult, if not impossible, to put forward a scientific definition of nationality. Initially what was meant by 'nationality' was the 'set of characteristics that constitute a nation' (p. 16); later the word was used to refer to a special collective formation. To avoid ambiguity van Gennep suggested the term 'nationalitarian' (*nationalitaire*).

Van Gennep observed that what seemed to defeat the majority of theoreticians who had tried to tackle the nationality question was the great variety and fluidity of its phenomenal forms. Most definitions of 'nationality', faced with the impossibility of agreeing about the list of elements which constitute it, abandoned any attempt to provide an objective, morphological approach to the matter and concluded that it was a fact of the collective consciousness; this reduction of nationality to a psychological phenomenon is the equivalent of saying that we cannot define what a nationality is; we can only ascertain that there is a 'nationalitarian way of thinking' *(manière de penser nationalitaire).* There is a tradition, which in France is identified with the work of Renan, that identifies the nationality with a phenomenon of collective psychology. Most authors who had written on nationality during the period of the First World War shared this conception. Van Gennep mentions, in particular, Henry Hauser's *Le Principe des nationalités*, Israel Zangwill's *The Principle of Nationalities* (1917), Bernard Auerbach's *Races et Nationalités d'Autriche-Hongrie* (1917) and René Johannet's *Le Principe des Nationalités* (1918). A great deal of the confusion exhibited by these authors stems from their inability to distinguish clearly between nationality and the State.

Van Gennep insists that nationality and State are different realities, which obey different principles. The State is a political reality, while it is possible to conceive of a nationality independently of the State. Just because France and a few other countries have a national identity which is clearly and historically associated with a State, it does not follow that the same should happen elsewhere. In fact, these countries are exceptions; Europe is a mosaic of nationalities. This we may not like, and from a practical point of view we might prefer that the population of Europe belonged to a single race, had a single language and had the same aspirations. However, 'we are left with a variety of groups which do not want to be assimilated to each other or to be absorbed by a single one of them' (p. 24). The objective of anthropology is to study, and if possible, to explain them (ibid.).

The author who seems to have come closest to van Gennep's vision of the nationality is the Bulgarian J. Ivanov, who defines it as

> a human collectivity, with a moral and physical individuality and with common traditions and aspirations. The elements that constitute and maintain the national individuality are: unity of race, geographic boundaries, language, religion, political unity, way of living and common cultural manifestations; the larger the number of these elements present in a nationality, the more its organisms are united and the more vigorous and ardent is the national sentiment that animates it. (p. 27)

Nonetheless, this definition, say van Gennep, lacks a reference to the conscious element, which is crucial in any definition of nationality. Furthermore, it is not sufficient to list the elements that constitute a nationality; it is important to know how they combine and what happens if one or more is absent.

According to van Gennep the sentiment of nationality already existed in pre-modern times. As he put it: 'a history of nationalitarian sentiment would be, properly speaking, a history of patriotism' (p. 33). Now, the latter takes different forms in accordance with the type of political organization in which it appears; in pre-modern times it was in the main dynastic; later on, at the time of the French Revolution, it became 'national' in the political sense of the term. But when we find a reasonably homogeneous human group which is unable to govern itself, and one of the key aspects of its collective consciousness is the will to self-determination, then we can talk about a 'nationalitarian' sentiment. What is modern is not the nationalitarian sentiment but the belief that a culturally defined group (van Gennep does not use this expression) has the natural right to govern itself. Of course, it is a fact that states have managed to create a sense of of patriotism out of culturally and linguistically diverse populations either through homogenization (France) or through the creation of state identity (Switzerland). In both cases, these were long-term processes, taking place over a few centuries. There is no doubt that what we see developing is a sense of loyalty towards the State (which becomes the *patrie* for peoples who might be otherwise culturally diverse).

Van Gennep is adamant that the nationalitarian sentiment precedes modernity, and he quotes a variety of cases in which the existence of such sentiment can be reasonably assumed. A particularly poignant document he refers to is that of the Polish scientist, Jacobus Szadek, who in 1464 laid down the basic nationalitarian principles. Claiming for the King of Poland, Kasimierz IV, the land of Pomerania (among others) from the Germans, he argued that it had been inhabited and governed by Polish people, who had given Polish names to mountains, rivers, towns, etc., long before the Teutonic Knights had existed. Furthermore, the lands had belonged to the Kingdom of Poland since its inception, and had been subject to Polish sovereignty. Finally, the argument was raised that the population of these lands could not be subjected to an oppressive, alien tyranny (p. 36).

It would appear that if the full expression of the principle of self-determination of peoples came only with the French Revolution, there are plenty of instances that suggest that it existed long before that time. In fact, what dominated the history of Europe since Roman times was what van Gennep called 'the Oriental conception of ethnic politics' (p. 39), which subordinated peoples to foreign rule. It was precisely the early anthropological development of an interest in ethnicity that contributed to highlighting the traditions of self-rule in the Celtic, Germanic and Slav worlds. In fact, these decentralizing traditions, which emphasized the rights to autonomy and freedom of cities, provinces, principalities and small kingdoms, never disappeared completely from the European horizon. Only with the advent of absolutism did this principle take a turn for the worse. It is on the basis of comparative human science that the European past can be recovered; the nationalitarian principle is a European legacy that was destroyed by an oppressive State modelled on the Oriental empires (p. 42). Van Gennep saw the emerging Soviet system as an extreme application of the Asiatic model, in that a heterogeneous mass of people was subjected to an alien oligarchy supported by a janissary army (the Bolsheviks).

Van Gennep defined colonialism as 'the application of the Oriental principle of domination to populations who are considered more or less civilized (due to the possession of more advanced means of destruction)'. He believed that the end of colonialism was near, and that this was due precisely to the spread of the nationalitarian principle to Asia and Africa. That the human sciences were not alien to these developments should be a source of pride for anthropologists (p. 43).

The application of the nationality principle will not suppress natural antagonisms, but perhaps will contribute to make massacres less common; at least one of the reasons for wars will be phased out. To what extent this principle might be a step backward from the universalism of the Enlightenment is one question that van Gennep asks himself. The idea of universal fraternity would possibly require the homogenization of languages, religions, political systems, etc. Only an evil empire could do that, and the Bolsheviks were the ideal candidates to try it. Van Gennep believed that the opposition between humanity and nationality is arbitrary, and that there is no reason why nationalities cannot live in peace with each other once they are free (p. 45).

I have already indicated that van Gennep did not manage to

articulate a comprehensive theory of nationality, and that at most he succeeded in mapping out the external factors that determine it.

There is, first, an outer layer of symbols of nationality which van Gennep just mentions. Traditionally, group differentiation was often achieved by means of manipulation of the body (tattoos, paintings, scarifications, mutilations, etc.); the modern equivalent of such procedures is national or regional dress. This is an easily distinguishable sign that allows a rapid classification of people in terms of friends or foes; it may also be used as a symbol of protest against an oppressive state. The process of European cultural homogenization has made dress a less relevant element of nationality, although in its folklorized form it still plays a certain role. The symbolic value attached to dress has been transferred in modern times to flags. Dress and flag are both about colours and about specific combinations of them (p. 53). The strong emotional value attached to flags as nationalitarian symbols (not only as military ones) finds no parallel in other elements. Whether the choice of flag be totally arbitrary or historically informed, a conscious decision is needed to adopt a given flag as the colours of a nationality. On the other hand, the spirit of a nationality may express itself through certain aspects of material culture, particularly the type of villages and houses (p. 56).

Among the controversial symbols of nationality van Gennep finds customs, traditions, rituals, etc. The reason is simply that some of these cultural manifestations cut across different countries; nonetheless, there is a sense in which people perceive them as theirs. Writing may also become a symbol of nationality, as is the case with the Serbs' and Croats' adopting different alphabets to transcribe their distinct, but closely related, languages. Van Gennep insisted that this issue was particularly relevant for Eastern Europe.

None of this outer layer of symbols of the nationality constitute either individually or collectively the core of the nationality. It has been shown that their disappearance does not mean the end of the 'emotive and reflective complex that constitutes the nationality' (p. 68). Among the external symbols of the nationality that van Gennep finds essential are language and territory.

Language is 'the most striking and pugnacious symbol of differentiation, continuity and collective cohesion' (ibid.). How early it was perceived that the existence of a variety of languages within the same state could be a cause of dissociation and how early the importance of language as a nationalitarian element was realized are topics that van Gennep explores in some detail. On the whole, he considers both as part of the thrust of modernity. I believe that he is wrong in that respect, and that we can find substantial manifestations of such occurrences prior to the dawn of modernity. Nonetheless, he is correct in emphasizing that the right of nationalities to preserve their language is a much more recent event, depending on 'the invention of the printing press, the establishment of linguistics as an autonomous discipline and the development of the railway system, which allowed for easy communications' (p. 73). These inventions were double-edged tools, which could be used both by the State and against the State. No doubt, the means at the disposal of the State to impose a language were far superior than those available to the oppressed nationalities (it was taught in schools and its use was made compulsory in the army, the administration, the judicial system, the press, etc.).

Van Gennep observed that the trend towards linguistic conformity that was predicted in the eighteenth century never materialized, and that the very opposite took place. The distinction between language, dialect and patois becomes more and more blurred; any dialect or patois can become, in the right circumstances, a nationalitarian language (p. 75). Nevertheless, small linguistic communities are always in danger of being absorbed by larger, linguistically close ones. Communities which speak closely connected languages tend to be in opposition to each other, because 'linguistic kinship appears to interested groups as a danger to their specific individuality' (p. 80). This may apply to dialects and patois as well. This opposition is the result of the fact that languages and dialects symbolize important psychological differences (p. 82).

Native, autochthonous languages are essentially an oral means to communicate at the familiar level, and hence strong emotions are attached to them. On the other hand, people may use other languages to engage in economic, social or political relations. Modern linguistic symbolism is the result of extending to the nationality what originally was typical of a smaller unit. In the absence of concerted action, administrative languages can displace native languages in a few generations if the economic needs or the state pressures are there. The importance of the mother tongue in determining nationality is exemplified by the use of official linguistic statistics. In the long run, linguistic censuses have accentuated the traits of both the dominant and the subordinated nationalities. The obsession of modern states with measuring the strength of maternal languages has been an important factor in highlighting the centrality of language in the constitution of the nationality. In van Gennep's words:

> If anything has contributed to spread among the masses the idea that the nationality is symbolized and recognized by the language, it is precisely the behaviour of governments in the elaboration of general or special censuses. By mid-nineteenth century the rural and urban masses did not clearly perceive this relationship. But the insistence of the census-takers on obtaining linguistic data and on influencing the answers, of governments on falsifying the results and of impassioned journalists, politicians and intellectuals on discussing them, has led to the idea, even in the most retarded countryside backyards, that to speak this or that language was to be in favour of or against the government. (p. 122)

Linguistic and other kinds of statistics are unreliable because they are open to easy manipulation by the State. Van Gennep offers a classic example of manipulation, which is as poignant today as it was seventy-five years ago. Macedonia is such an example. He looks at the claims of Bulgarians, Serbs and Greeks concerning this area. Bulgarians take language (without distinguishing between maternal language and language of use), religion (declaration of attachment to the Bulgarian exarchate Church) and the declaration of nationality as the basic facts of national consciousness. For Serbs what counts are the basic facts of dialect and spoken language, the resemblance of customs and religion. Finally, Greeks consider the so-called influence of Hellenic civilization, as it manifests itself in all sort of survivals (from the belief in vampires to the use of specialized Greek words, from popular tales to dress), as the decisive factor. Who, then, are, the Macedonians; are they Greeks, Bulgarians or Serbs? Or are they just Macedonians? The answer was as problematic when van Gennep was writing as it is today (p. 125). One must therefore conclude that the nationality is an entity which is too complex and dynamic to be enclosed in the confines of a statistical approach (p. 143).

Another symbol of group cohesion and persistence, as powerful as the linguistic one, is the territory (p. 143). This association between a people and a territory is not exclusively a modern phenomenon. Patriotic sentiments tend to develop as a result of the attachment of human beings to a particular land; these localized sentiments can be extended to the whole territory of the State or of the nationality. Oral and written literature have often expressed the force of the territorial symbolism. There are, of course, some cases of nationalities without a territory (the Gypsies, for example), but they are rare. The Jews, maintains van Gennep, are not one of them, because they have an ancestral territory and a strong symbolic association with it.

Closely associated with the territory is the problem of borders. 'Territory only acquires its full symbolic value when we know its boundaries' (p. 151). The idea of boundary exists in all societies from primitive to civilized. Different markers have been used to indicate boundaries: some natural, others artificial. These markers are often envisaged as sacred; to cross a boundary is to move from one world to another; it represents performing magic and a religious ritual. Often, limits are invisible: the ideal line traced between two physical markers; the 'symbol of the border' is a secondary symbol within the nationality sentiment (p. 152). The precision in delineating borders is a recent thing; in the past what was common was not an ideal line, or even a clearly defined geographic marker (river, mountain, etc.), but rather a frontier, a border area which was neutral (No Man's Land). Marches also belonged in this category. In any case, van Gennep criticizes the concept of 'natural borders', as well as the idea of natural linguistic borders. Neither mountains, nor rivers, nor seas nor forests are an obstacle for the expansion of a language. Van Gennep dedicates Chapters 7 and 8 of the book to tackling these issues.

In the context of the discussion on borders a number of related, important concepts appeared in the nineteenth century. Ideas like access to the sea, control of water sources, military strategy ('safe borders'), economic borders, etc. Van Gennep is convinced that the attempt by geographers to discover a causal link or a normal coincidence between nationalitarian or political boundaries, on the one hand, and natural boundaries, on the other, has failed. The concentration, dispersion and expansion of peoples follows its own logic, and it is not the geographic one, except in rare and passing circumstances (p. 174). Borders are changing symbols of human relationships. The attempt to correlate nationalitarian borders and geographic ones has created many political problems in the nineteenth and twentieth centuries.

The importance of the cartographic symbol, spread by school maps, is also remarked on by van Gennep. There is a patriotic feeling of pride in imperial maps (like those showing the British Empire in red). But ethnographic maps tend to be rather unreliable, often providing mixed information. In addition to the linguistic element, the nationalitarian border also incorporates other elements which are ethnographic (customs and buildings), psychological (religion, collective will), economic and strategic. Along with all these factors one must also consider the idea of historical borders, which van Gennep considered a dangerously volatile concept (p. 207).

Van Gennep introduces the idea of historical symbol to refer to the 'image that each people has of its past military and political greatness, an image which was traditionally perpetuated by heroic legends, war songs, live memories, etc., and that today is transmitted in uncritical history textbooks and illustrated with maps'.

Another important symbol is the name of the nationality (territory and inhabitants). Names come, go and return. At the time of writing his book van Gennep observed that names such as Serbs, Croats and Slovenes (which had existed for a thousand years) were being phased out and replaced by that of Yugoslavs; now the very opposite is happening. Some names of nations are rooted in past peoples with whom there is no ethnic or cultural link (Angles and English, Franks and French, etc.) Sometimes the names of territories remain unchanged, but the peoples who inhabit them change. The symbolic importance of the name is a survival from earlier times; the name is the most powerful symbol of the cohesion and the persistence of the group as an organized collectivity. Andrew Lang based on this essential value of the collective name his theory of the origins of totemism, and hence of religious and social organization. 'Deutschland über alles' and 'Rule Britannia' are but abridged formulae of the sentiment and image of the name. In modern times there is a tendency to favour a coincidence between the name of territory and that of its inhabitants: Poland is the land of the Poles, etc. Old, multinational countries fit rather badly in this scheme (p. 213).

The book concludes with the idea that

> the superposition, and in favourable cases, the combination of all symbols analysed determine in the individuals and in the masses the

> formation of a tangible (sensible) representation of their nationality. This representation contains visual, auditive and sensorial elements, to which are added other more or less conscious and nuanced sentiments, according to the degree of individual and collective sensibility and education. (p. 217)

Van Gennep observed that symbols may lose part of their importance, particularly when the nationality is well established; on the other hand, nationalitarian symbols do not acquire their full value until the nationality is in danger or at war.

As I have indicated at the beginning, van Gennep's treatise stops at the external manifestations of the nationality; it provides only, as he put it, a plastic representation. However, it lacks a consideration of the internal materials from which the nationality is formed, how these materials are assembled and the framework that sustains them and keeps them in place. Without these it is very difficult to discern the general law which determines the origins, conduct and evolution of the nationality.

Marcel Mauss

There is little doubt that Marcel Mauss's interest in the national question was awakened by the nationalist turmoils associated with the First World War. As with van Gennep, his interest in the matter seems to have fizzled out a few years later. Mauss's main text on the national question – *La Nation* (1920) – is, as I have already noted, much shorter and less coherent (because it is made up of disparate fragments) than van Gennep's *Traité Comparatif des Nationalités*. The editor of the manuscript, H. Lévy-Bruhl, emphasizes three main characteristics : (1) it is written in the grand style, and aims to be a comprehensive and monumental treatise; (2) it tries to capture two nationalitarian trends, which are only contradictory in apperance, that is, fissiparity and union; and (3) while noting the importance of economic factors in the making of the nation, Mauss also takes on board elements like politics, language, religion and morality (Lévy-Bruhl 1953–4: 7). Unlike van Gennep, Mauss focuses on the nation, rather than the nationality, and envisages it as a total phenomenon. Now, nation and State are quite close in Maussian terminology, though the former is less juridical and more emotive than the latter (1969a: 572).

The nation, as an eighteenth-century concept, is constituted by the citizens of the State. This is essentially a French concept which developed with the Enlightenment, and more specifically with Rousseau, and culminated in the French Revolution. The concept of nation comes much later to the English tradition, which only knows of 'subjects', 'kingdom' and 'country', and thinks of the nation in these terms. Even the American revolutionaries were not altogether aware of the national character of their actions.

Here Mauss pinpoints a difference in national character between the English and Continentals (or at least French and Germans); while among the former the law precedes concepts and ideas, with the latter the opposite is the case (Mauss 1969a: 374–5). Patriotism *stricto sensu* flourished only in the context of the nation politically understood. Mauss is quite adamant that neither fidelity to the king (nor loyalty to the State) nor the hatred of foreign rulers can be equated with patriotism. What is at stake in modern, proper patriotism is its popular character. As he put it:

'Nations in formation, like Italy and Germany, and even more oppressed nationalities, like Poland, Bohemia, Hungary and Serbia, developed in succession a consciousness of their will to exist, to revolt and to reconstitute themselves . . . And the nationality principle expressed symbolically this claim of nations to existence, to a complete existence' (ibid.: 575–6).

It would appear that in the course of the nineteenth century the concept of nation understood as the will of the people lost popularity in favour of the concepts of nationality and State; the former emphasizes the revolt against alien domination, the latter empties out society of its citizens.

Mauss's objective is to investigate which type of society can be labelled nation. In that he follows the Aristotelian distinction between *ethnē* (peoples) and *poleis* (states or nations). What determines the difference between *ethnos* and *polis* is the lack of integration and solidarity which characterizes the former. Nations show a high degree of vertebration and consciousness of themselves, which is absent or poorly developed in peoples. The imagery used by Mauss is biological, although he is aware of the dangers, and after a *tour de force* he arrives at the following definition of the nation:

'A nation is a society materially and morally integrated, with a centralized power which is stable and permanent, with clearly delimited borders, and with a relative moral, mental and cultural unity of its inhabitants, who consciously adhere to a state and its laws' (p. 584).

As can be seen, this is a rather restrictive definition of the nation, and makes of it a rather recent institution. The nation is thus essentially a Western European product, and it requires the following two conditions:

1. Society has to be integrated: that is, all segmentation by clan, city, tribe, kingdom or feudality has to be abolished. Ideally, there are no intermediaries between the nation and the citizen. In addition to that, nations have clear boundaries, without areas which depend on foreign rulers and without designs on the territory of other nations.

2. There must be economic unity. The idea of a national economy is essential for Mauss; economic life flows as far as the boundaries of the nation. The members of a nation are unified economically; protectionism and nationalism often coincide. A good case in point of economic nationalism was the creation of a national market as a precondition for the creation of a political nation in Germany in the nineteenth century.

The question arises as to whether these two factors are sufficient to define the nation. Mauss seems to answer in the negative, by saying the following:

> But this political unity, that is to say, military, administrative and juridical, on the one hand, and economic, on the other, and especially this conscious, constant, general will to create it and to transmit it to all and sundry, has only become possible by means of a series of considerable phenomena which have unified the other social phenomena, either at the same time, or before or after. A nation which deserves to be called a nation has its civilization, aesthetic, moral and material, and its language. It has its mentality, its sensibility, its morality, its will and its form of progress; and all the citizens who compose the nation participate in the Idea that directs her. (p. 591)

The process of individuation of nations and nationalities has taken place in the past two centuries; civilization has not become more uniform, but rather the opposite.

> This local, moral and juridical unity is expressed in the collective spirit by the idea of fatherland, on the one hand, and by the idea of citizen, on the other. The idea of fatherland symbolizes the sum total of duties that citizens have *vis-à-vis* the nation and its land. The notion of the citizen symbolizes the sum total of civil and political rights that the member of this nation has in correlation with the duties that he must accomplish. (p. 592)

These two ideas constitute the modern nation; the nation, for Mauss, is made up of citizens who live consensually.

In a modern nation the tendency is to individualize its members and reduce them to uniformity; the nation is homogeneous, like a primitive clan, and it consists of equal citizens. It is symbolized by its flag, while the clan had its totem. The nation has its cult, as the clan worshipped its ancestral god-animals. Like a primitive tribe, the nation has its dialect elevated to the dignity of a language, and it has its domestic law, which is opposed to international law. Like a clan, the nation claims the right to vendetta when offended. The nation has its own currency, customs, borders and colonies; even mentality and race are marked by individuation (p. 594).

Mauss insists that this process of individuation of the nation is visible even in two very different, unexpected orders of phenomena: in the higher forms of intellectual life (*mentalité*) and in the forms of biological life (*race*). The use of a given language, with its traditions, characteristics, literary forms, etc., contributes to individuate the nation to a hitherto unforeseen extent. The scientific literature often misses this process, because either it is only predicated of primitive societies (which are then envisaged as nations) or because the homogenization of the modern world is assumed (p. 594). According to Mauss, modern European nations believe in their common race, no matter how erroneous this conception might be – after all, European populations are racially mixed. There are constant references to the French or the English race in the nationalist literature. And for many, race creates nationality (though in fact the opposite is the case).

An important phenomenon which is typical of the nineteenth century is the creation of national languages by nationalities that did not previously have them. This usually applies to peoples who had unwritten or forgotten languages. Language has often preceded nationality. What we can see here is 'a will of the people to intervene in processes which until recently had been left to unconscious variations and developments' (p. 598). For Mauss this should not be seen as 'artificialism'; linguistic nationalism is a strong sentiment, and peoples want to colour European culture with their language. In modern times language has created the nationality. States often want to impose the dominant language on populations with different languages; but the fact that this is felt as an imposition shows the progress that the principle of the autonomy of peoples has made (p. 599).

Finally, for Mauss a nation believes in its civilization, in its mores, in its technology and in its art. Nations have a high opinion of themselves, believing perhaps to be the most civilized and the best in the world. After this examination of different factors Mauss proposes a final, more sophisticated definition of the nation as 'a sufficiently integrated society, with central power (at least democratic to a certain degree), with the idea of national sovereignty and the boundaries of which are those of a race, a civilization, a language, a morality, in a word, a national character'. Of course, some elements may be absent, but in the complete nation all these elements coincide. There are few examples of complete nations (France being one of them), and Mauss believes these to be aesthetically more appealing.

Conclusion

In this chapter I have merely tried to present what I believe to be a wealth of anthropological analyses on the national question that have hitherto remained unexplored. If not an elaborate theory of the nation or of nationality, I think there are brilliant insights, finely tuned comparisons and detailed analyses in both authors. It should be said that van Gennep and Mauss approached the national question historically and with an ethnographic richness (in relation to both Western and Eastern Europe) that my paper has not been able to reflect appropriately. I have not been able to trace any reference to the work of van Gennep on nationality in the anthropological literature (or in the literature on the national question in general). As to Mauss, his definition of the nation was taken up by L. Dumont (1970); Dumont also elaborated Mauss's idea of moral integration to mean that the nation should be seen both as collection of individuals and as a whole. R. Grillo (1980) also quotes the Maussian text approvingly, but goes no further.

In a programmatic article published some years ago I stated that the tasks of a theory of nationalism in Europe involved three major objectives: (a) an understanding of the subjective sentiments of national identity, as well as the associated elements of consciousness; (b) an account of the genesis and evolution of the idea of nation from the medieval period to early modern times; and (c) a spatio-temporal explanation of the varying structures (ideologies and movements) of nationalism in the modern and contemporary periods (Llobera 1987).

If we consider who are the best-known contemporary anthropologists who have studied the national question in Europe, the names of Gellner and Dumont spring to mind. In some respects their approaches are very different, but they are equally innovative. Methodologically speaking, their approaches could be construed as exemplary, particularly for those anthropologists who are still pussyfooting around the verandas of their village 'communities'.

Although I believe that there are limitations and anomalies in Gellner's theory, he has gone a long way in providing a reasoned account for the emergence and pervasiveness of nationalism in modern times (Gellner 1983). His idea that the roots of nationalism are found in the specific structural needs of industrial society has appealed to a wide range of anthropologists (as well as social scientists). Gellner's insistence that nations are invented has also been widely accepted, among other things because, like the previous thesis, it confirms the generalized perception among many social scientists that nationalism is best explained in economic terms. However, Gellner has little to say about national sentiments and consciousness; in fact, this is a topic that social scientists have largely ignored. The work of van Gennep, but also the Durkheimian tradition in general, can be of assistance in providing a number of elements with which to build a theory of national consciousness. A rich and specific contribution stemming from van Gennep's book is his treatment of the symbols of nationality and their relationship to the creation of national consciousness. Again, for some unspecified reason the Durkheimians made little use of the concepts of collective consciousness and collective representations outside the realm of primitive societies, although Mauss recognized their wider applicability. A projection into modern society of some of the analytic frameworks used in *Les formes élémentaires de la vie religieuse* could help to clarify the meaning and importance of nationalist beliefs and rituals.

L. Dumont, who places himself in the Durkheimian tradition, has published a series of articles on the German and French national ideologies (Dumont 1986, 1991) which are much more limited in scope than Gellner's book. His writings have so far only influenced a limited but fervent and influential circle of anthropological admirers. By focusing on some key philosophical and literary texts, Dumont has claimed to have uncovered three basic principles of the German mind (universal sovereignty, introverted individualism and holism) which are the key to modernity. Dumont remains prisoner of the conviction that one can explain historical developments as complex as Nazism without reference to macro historico-sociological categories (Llobera, forthcoming).

A comparison between Gellner and Dumont highlights the limited explanatory framework of the élitist cultural structuralism of Dumont as against the sociological structuralism of Gellner. To be sure, Gellner's approach is also history-bereft, and that is its major scientific weakness. There is a sense, then, in which the Durkheimian tradition, seen through the eyes of Lévi-Straussian structuralism, can generate concise and elegant models that unfortunately have little connection to a reality that is historically much richer and more complex. What was perhaps acceptable for societies 'without history', is totally inappropriate for modern Europe. In some ways it is interesting to emphasize that both van Gennep and Mauss, but particularly the former, are much more concerned with history than our two contemporary anthropologists.

At a time when the collapse of the Communist régimes, the building of a united Europe and the weakening of the pseudo nation-states has put the national question once more in the foreground, I think that there is much that we can learn from the writings of van Gennep and Mauss.

References

Dumont, L. (1970) [1964]. Nationalism and Communalism. In *Religion, Politics and History in India* (ed. L. Dumont), Paris: Mouton.

Dumont, L. (1986). *Essays on Individualism*, Chicago: Chicago University Press.
Dumont, L. (1991). *L'idéologie allemande* Paris, Gallimard.
Gellner, E. (1983). *Nations and Nationalism*, Oxford: Blackwell.
Grillo, R. (1980). Introduction to *Nation and State in Europe* (ed. R. Grillo), New York: Academic Press.
Halbwachs, M. (1980). *The Collective Memory*, New York: Harper and Row.
Halbwachs, M. (1992) *On Collective Memory*, Chicago: Chicago University Press.
Lévy-Bruhl, H. (1953–4) Avertissement, *L'Année Sociologique*, troisième série: 5–7.
Llobera, J. R. (1987). Nationalism: Some Methodological Issues. *JASO*, **18**, (1), 13–25.
Llobera, J. R. (1994). Durkheim and the National Question. In *Debating Durkheim* (eds H. Martins and S. W. F. Pickering). London: Routledge.
Llobera, J. R. (forthcoming) The German Conception of the Nation. A Critique of L. Dumont's Writings on the German Question.
Mauss, M. (1969a). La nation. In *Oeuvres*, Paris: Minuit, Vol III: 573–625.
Mauss, M. (1969b). La nation et l'internationalisme. In *Oeuvres*. Paris: Minuit. Vol III: 626–39.
Van Gennep, A. (1920). La Nationalité géorgienne. Les causes de sa formationet de son maintien, *Revue de l'Institut de Sociologie Solvay*, 1re année, no. 3: 7–46.
Van Gennep, A. (1921a). Classe rural, noblesse et nationalité, *Revue de l'Institut de Sociologie Solvay*, 2e année, no.1: 200–22.
Van Gennep, A. (1921b). L'action du sol sur la formation des Nationalités, *Le Monde Nouveau*, 3e année, III: 1659–72.
Van Gennep, A. (1922a). *Traité comparatif des Nationalités. Les éléments extérieurs de la Nationalité*, Paris: Payot.
Van Gennep, A. (1922b). Religion et Nationalité, *Journal de Psychologie Normale et Pathologique*, 19e année, Janvier: 24–46.

Chapter 5

'Fortress Europe' and the Foreigners Within: Germany's Turks

Ruth Mandel

In this chapter I address a number of issues relating to questions of identity and boundaries – physical and social – affecting the population of migrants from Turkey in Germany. As a result of the end of the Cold War, the collapse of the Berlin Wall, and the unification of Germany, the situation of non-citizen foreign migrants has changed. The redrawing of the geopolitical map of Eastern and Central Europe necessitates a rethinking of domestic German relations as well. Thus, though most of my research was carried out in pre-unification Germany, I will touch on the current unified climate as well. But as so often happens with research of this sort, and particularly in this part of the world, history has caught up with, if not overtaken, the ethnography.

In the mid and late 1980s I spent over two years living in Berlin carrying out ethnographic research, primarily among the Turkish migrant community. West Berlin at that time was something of an overdetermined city-state, heavily symbolic of an array of contradictions. Physically surrounded by the German Democratic Republic, West Berlin stood at once for Western decadence and promiscuous consumption, as well as the 'free world' and Western liberal democracy. Encoded in innumerable ways, these ideas were broadcast to the Communist east twenty-four hours a day on the US military's Armed Forces Radio, as well as the national German television channels and radio stations. Most West Berliners accepted the Wall as an inevitable fact of life, and had little concern with or interest in what went on beyond it.

But even in the indifference shown it, the Wall helped to shape the preciousness of the *Zeitgeist* and culture that for many represented West Berlin. Divided into three sectors, West Berlin was ruled by a bizarre set of laws, customs and regulations, devised by the Allies after the Second World War. Artificially propped up by financial assistance from the West German government, the West Berlin economy was not otherwise viable. Now, all this has changed dramatically. The enormous US military presence will be gone by 1994. Traces of the Wall and the strip of no-man's-land alongside it are being erased at breakneck speed, in the massive urban renewal projects. (Berlin is perhaps the one spot in the Western world where the construction industry has not been devastated by the recession.) Two very separate countries have been merged together, not so much as equals, but, as the popular expression has it, as the West German colonization of East Germany. In many respects, East German society, identity and political culture have been forcibly eliminated. In the 'five new states', as the former GDR is now called, this has caused a national identity crisis and collective cognitive dissonance on a unprecedented scale. There has been a wholesale dismantling of the education system, the bureaucracy, the organization of recycling, the entire medical system based on polyclinics – in short, every aspect of life as it was known. In addition, on an individual level, eastern Germans who now operate in western environments must deal with the psychological pressures of sticking out, of being the 'bad' easterners, of having the wrong accents, taste, clothing, work ethics, habits, and the like.

Furthermore, the eastern Germans for the most part have been accustomed to life in an ethnically homogeneous society. Now they, especially those in Berlin, or those who live in close proximity to foreigner (often refugee) hostels, for the first time must deal with people they perceive as very different from them.

One of the most vexing problems facing the new and enlarged Germany is the question of the foreigners within. It has become increasingly apparent that now there are several classes of outsiders, or foreigners (in German, one word, *Auslander* describes both; see Forsythe 1989). Before unification the salient social identity opposition was between German and *Auslander* – usually a euphemism for Turk. Now, a new set of identities has emerged – Western vs. Eastern people. As mentioned above, the very real differences between them are manifested in a myriad of forms: in disparate sensibilities and experiences, as well as their separate and unequal economic situations and vocational prospects.

However, in many ways cross-cutting these formidable differences are the Turkish migrant workers and their families. On the one hand the Turks are more 'foreign' than the Germans of the eastern 'new states', yet in many cases the Turks are much better integrated into the western German social and economic structures. Consequently, they have become victimized, as they serve as targets for the anger, frustration and violence of some desperate, often eastern Germans.

A Historical Precedent

The contemporary period is not the first time that labour migration has been a controversial issue in Germany. In the late nineteenth and early twentieth centuries, between 1870 and 1914, industrialization in the west encouraged migration from the east (Bade 1987). German agricultural labourers from the *Junker* landed estates in the eastern regions moved to newly industrialized western areas. Consequently, Poles began to move *en masse* to fill the agricultural jobs. This period was marked by dramatic demographic shifts in the agricultural and industrial sectors. Whereas the German economy had been primarily agricultural until the mid-nineteenth century, by 1871 the rural segment had dropped to 64 per cent of the population; by 1900 it was 46 per cent, and the decrease continued thereafter. Between 1882 and 1907 the number of workers employed in industry rose from 4.1 million to 8.6 million, or by 110 per cent, while the actual population only increased from 45.2 million to 61.7 million, or by 37 per cent (Rhoades 1978: 556). The first wave of Polish migrants came for seasonal, agricultural work.

> By 1890, seasonal agricultural workers were required to register with the police and return to their home country during the winter off-season. The return trip, however, could be avoided simply by renewing the identification card. Many aliens, however, remained illegally in Germany without fulfilling this requirement. Although work contracts always stipulated that employment was seasonal, this rule was strictly enforced only during periods of recession. (p. 556)

Later the Poles moved into the industrial sectors further west, and many worked in the mining areas both in Germany and in Belgium.

By 1913 in the Ruhr region (Germany's central industrial area, then as now) there were 1,177 Polish associations. Polish banks, churches, newspapers, and trade unions flourished, to the point that, as early as 1886, 'cries of *Überfremdung* ('over-foreignization') arising from nationalist sentiment brought Bismarck to expel thirty thousand Polish workers and temporarily halt immigration' (p. 557; see also Brubaker 1992). In 1908 public use of the Polish language was banned, which led to the bizarre phenomenon of '"dumb assemblies" . . . in which nobody said a word, but [at which] leaflets in Polish were read communally' (Castles and Kosack 1973: 20).

Max Weber, in his *Antrittsrede* (inaugural address) of 1885, upon his appointment as Professor of Economics in Freiburg, asserted that the influx of Polish workers from the east threatened the hegemony of German culture where it had been strongest, among the *Junker* landowners. He called for the immigration to cease and the borders to be secured (Giddens 1972: 11; cf. also the Heidelberg Manifesto 1981).

Until 1905 employers hired workers informally, privately. In 1905 the Deutsche Feldarbeiterzentrale (later the Deutsche Arbeiterzentrale), had emerged, which were agencies in the federal government (Rhoades 1978: 558). The latter were 'the precursor of the present Bundesanstalt für Arbeit, the Federal Labour Office, that still, in conjunction with sending-country agencies, recruits and selects workers' (p. 259).

In the 1910 census 1,259,880 foreigners and 64,935,993 Germans lived in Germany (Krane 1975: 65).[1] The official term by which the foreigners were designated was *Reichsausländer*; they were residents but not citizens. Though there was a significant repatriation of Poles, many did remain and assimilate into the surrounding population. In Germany today it is not uncommon to encounter Polish surnames, particularly in regions that once had major Polish worker populations. This historical precedent is used in revisionist arguments frequently made about the present Turkish migrants. Ignorant of the history, until recently some Germans complained about the high profile of the Turks and the associated

1. Compare with 2.2 million foreigners employed in West Germany in 1974.

'foreigner problems' in terms of the Poles: 'Why can't the Turks just settle in and assimilate like the Poles did?' Now, with the new wave of ethnic Polish-'German' immigrants, the xenophobia has become more complex.

Castles tells us that 'as late as 1960 West Germany had no significant number of non-European residents. During the sixties large numbers of Turkish workers were recruited, so that by 1970 469,000 (or 16 per cent) of the nearly 3 million foreign residents were Turks' (1984: 75). With the halt of labour recruitment in 1973 the demographic composition of the migrant community began to change. Male workers, having overstayed their initial short-term residence, started to bring their families. The foreign population rose with the birth rate, so that 'by 1975 there were more non-employed foreigners than employed' (p. 74). In addition the national composition was changing, as Greek and Spanish migrants saw that repatriation was increasingly attractive, as their countries' economies began to develop and the respective military dictatorships collapsed (Spain: 1975; Greece: 1974).

'Foreigners' and Refugees

It should be stressed that a large portion of these 'foreigners' were born in, and have grown up in Germany. The confluence of German laws of citizenship and ideologies of ethnicity, nation and state, have effectively prevented this population from achieving legal and social equality, and civil rights, by denying them crucial access to full citizenship. This must be viewed in the context of the granting of full citizenship – quite literally overnight – to all of the citizens of the former East German state, as well as to the so-called 'ethnic Germans' from East European countries such as Poland, Czechoslovakia and Romania. Proof of a German ancestor who resided within the 1937 boundaries of the German Reich has been sufficient to claim German citizenship today. Perhaps it is not so surprising that acceptable evidence for this is a grandparent's membership card in the Nazi Party. Thus, descendants of card-carrying Nazis, in most cases monolingual Poles, have an automatic 'bloodright' to German citizenship, but *not* necessarily the second- and third-generation descendants of Turkish migrant workers, born and reared in Germany. The irony is glaringly apparent when one looks at Germany's history of Polish immigration.

The disturbing escalation of xenophobic violence, sometimes fatal, aimed at Turks and other foreigners, particularly in the districts of the former East Berlin and a number of regions of the former German Democratic Republic, is indicative of growing tensions that have yet to be resolved. The well-publicized, violent riot organized by (east) German neo-Nazis at the refugee shelters in Saxon Hoyerswerda in the summer of 1992 was seen by many as merely the tip of an iceberg; their fears were later confirmed with the murder of 3 Turks in Molln and 5 Turks in Solingen, all the victims of arson attacks.

Furthermore, not unproblematically, the German government's reaction mildly echoes the radical right – their explicit policy, that 'the boat is full', paves the way for even more restrictive immigration legislation. Germany's new asylum law, a virtual dismantling of Article 16 of the constitution, fundamentally changes the nature and practice of asylum in Europe. Before the recent constitutional changes this spring, Germany served as the country with the most liberal asylum policy in Europe, accepting 60 per cent of all asylum applicants in the EC. This was a remnant of moral reparations or compensation after the Second World War; in some senses, it was a recognition of collective culpability for the ethnic cleansing carried out by the German National Socialist state. Now, one consequence of the political unification of the two German states has been to revoke this liberal stance. In effect, this can be understood as the State's more than symbolic endorsement of, if not capitulation to, the right-extremist agenda of '*Ausländer raus*' – foreigners out.

However, despite what on paper was in fact a liberal asylum policy, most applicants for asylum have been denied. The figures in December 1992 showed that 1,516,000 persons had taken refuge in Germany, of whom 1,286,000 were in that liminal status of being stateless foreigners, *de facto* refugees under threat of being sent away, or asylum applicants. Of the more than one-and-one-half million foreign refugees, only 100,000 or 6.6 per cent had been granted asylum (Federal Government Foreign Affairs Division 1993: 63).

Foreigners of a different sort from the refugees, the status of the nearly two million resident Turkish citizens and other non-German foreign resident migrant workers and their families is becoming ever more precarious. Though they lack the right to become citizens, most are legal residents.[2] Many have lived there since the early 1960s, when Germany recruited them for needed manual labour to fuel the post-war boom economy. Between 1960 and 1973, when the international oil crisis brought recruitment to a grinding halt, over one million workers were brought into Germany. Since that time, the numbers have grown, due to the reproduction of a second and now a third generation, offsetting those who have repatriated.

German unification has rendered many aspects of the lives of the migrants insecure. In addition to the openly hostile environment and violence, there have been major changes in the shape and meaning of living space. For example, the well-known 'Turkish ghetto', Kreuzberg, before unification was located at the periphery of the city, surrounded on three sides by East Berlin and the Wall. The most dilapidated quarter of the Western, American sector, it was little changed since the War. Its rents were kept low, as the cold-water apartments often lacked inside toilets and central heating. Now, Kreuzberg's identity has changed, as it finds itself in the centre of a larger and unified Berlin, vulnerable to encroaching eager real estate speculators, gentrifiers and violent gangs of neo-Nazi youth from the east, now only a few subway train stops away.

Germany has yet to come to terms with this sizeable foreign population within the context of its own new identity. The government, for years having denied that the labour migrants were permanent immigrants, must now account for what seems to be an intractable problem between its disgruntled citizens from the former German Democratic Republic and the resident foreigners.

2. As of 1991 the Foreign Residents Act was changed to include the following groups of persons having a right to naturalization: (1) foreigners between the ages 16 and 23 who have lived in Germany on a regular basis for a period of at least eight years and have attended a school in Germany for a period of at least six years; (2) foreigners of 24 years or older who have lived in Germany on a regular basis for a period of at least 15 years and are able to make a living for themselves and their families; (3) spouses and children (minors) of foreigners of 24 years of age or older having lived in Germany on a regular basis for at least 15 years.

The obvious problems with this liberalized naturalization law are first, that a common pattern for the second generation youth has been to be shuffled back and forth between Turkey and Germany throughout their childhood; this could easily exclude a large share of the foreign youth. Second, 'are able to make a living' can be subject to interpretation. Since the recession, three times as many Turks have been made redundant as Germans; to be able to make a living and to be able to find a job are two entirely different things.

Turkey in and out of Europe

Long an affiliate member of the European Community, Turkey has been juggling with its liminal east–west identity since the mid-Ottoman Empire (see e.g. B. Lewis 1961). On such fundamental issues as rights of residence, work and travel, this incomplete affiliation is of critical importance. In this section of the chapter I examine the meanings of this marginality, and compare the different consequences of relative 'European-ness' for labour migrants in Germany.

In Germany the migrant workers from Turkey, who have been known colloquially and collectively as *Gastarbeiter*, guestworkers, are not welcomed by Germans as fellow Europeans. Nor are they welcomed any longer as guests. They are associated with the *Morgenland,* land of the morning, the orient – the implicit opposition is with the [more mature] *Abendland,* the occident, the west. Clearly, the twin concepts are ordered hierarchically.

In Germany the image of the Turk is frequently objectified and essentialized. And, the essentializing generalizations distance them beyond the embrace of Europeanness. This leaves them pushed to the margins, their identity being relegated to that of permanent outsiders. One of the central problems in terms of claiming a legitimate locally-based identity is the seeming absence of a conceptual space (inside the social margins) for a group that might claim to be separate and different but equal.

However, just as clear divisions between segments of the German population can be identified, parallels within the foreign community are found as well. First, reproducing the Germans' perception, the many nationalities place themselves within a hierarchically ordered scheme. Christian European *Gastarbeiter* clearly rank at the top. Italians, Greeks and what were once Yugoslavs compose this group. Spaniards and Portuguese, though less numerous, also would be ranked here. Italians would probably be at the top of the pecking order. The more distant and different from German society – in terms of social, cultural and physical proxemics – the further down a group finds itself. That the Turks occupy the lowest rung is indicated linguistically – as mentioned above, the word 'Turk' has come to be synonymous with *Ausländer*, foreigner, outsider. Among the various migrant groups, internal differentiation is also apparent. For example, urban Turks from Western Turkey often feel little if any kinship with their poorer rural compatriots. Worse yet, from the perspective of some, are the Kurds from Eastern Anatolia, whom they regard as little better than primitive. The self-designated 'Westernized' urban Turks often feel shame and resentment towards their 'backwards, embarrassing' compatriots, who, they say, give *all* Turks, 'even the well-integrated, modern ones' a bad name. Some also blame them for the considerable *yabancî düsmanligi – Ausländer-feindlichkeit* (prejudice, ill-will, stereotyping and xenophobia) most migrants claim to experience.

The migrants from Greece stand in a marginally better position in German society. At least in part this is due to the fact that Germans trace their intellectual heritage to Greece (albeit the Greece of 2,500 years ago). Germany produced schools of classical Greek philology, and Goethe was much enamoured with Greece, idealized it and translated modern (nineteenth-century) Greek folk songs. Furthermore, Greece has been for many years an established favourite vacation spot for Germans, growing numbers of whom own property there and return annually. The vacation potential of Turkey, on the other hand, has only more recently been discovered by German tourists; thus, the familiarity of Greece is far greater than that of Turkey to many Germans. Also, Greek music and food are well known and appreciated in West Germany. Moreover, Greece has been an almost-full member of the European Community since January 1981: the economic links symbolize a sense of inclusion into Europe that Turkey lacks.

In Greece the most salient 'other' has nearly always been the Turk, to the extent that Greekness is often conceived of in direct opposition to imagined and feared Turkishness. But in Germany the labels, treatment, and concepts of *Auslander* and 'Turk' are frequently used synonymously and interchangeably, and it is therefore surprising and confusing, if not highly upsetting, for Greeks to be mistaken for and called 'Turks'. The situation elicits novel reactions and responses, from a critical rethinking and re-evaluation of the traditional nationalist, acutely anti-Turkish animosity, to the Greeks' wholesale appropriation of the dominant culture's values and attitudes about Turks (cf. Herzfeld 1987: 107).

Insiders, Outsiders, Citizens

The objectification of the Turks, as mentioned above, contributes to their marginalized status. It also continues to mark them as an unassimilable 'other', by affirming an essential difference between the 'foreigners/Turks' and 'us'. This is clear not only in the rhetoric deployed by the right-wing politicians and neo-Nazis, who are clear in their agenda for Turks to repatriate. The liberal civil-rights-minded groups, as well, use language that serves to separate, and treat as other, the Turks and other non-Germans. This is not unrelated to the twin ideologies of nation and citizen, guided by the native notion of ethnicity.

In a statement by Chancellor Helmut Kohl, given at a cabinet meeting in 1992, he said of the foreign workers, 'We want to live together as friends and neighbours' . . . the coda he implied, by neglecting to add it, was 'but not as citizens'. This is because the German law recognizes the powerful symbol of blood, in the form of German ancestry and ethnicity, as the basic criterion for citizenship.

The pervasiveness of the term *Auslander*, having replaced *Gastarbeiter* in many contexts, reinforces the marginal role of the Turks, be they first, second or third generation in Germany. Another term, *Mitburger*, co- or fellow-citizen, can be heard as well, particularly among well-meaning politicians and in certain sectors of the public. The collocation 'foreign co-/fellow-citizen', marks even more an already marked population in a way that 'real' unmarked citizens – citizens without the *Mit-* prefix – are not. One does not hear of German Protestants or Bavarians singled out as co-citizens. The simple prefix *Mit-*, used to indicate euphemistic inclusion by those to whom *Auslander* sounds too harsh, instead highlights the fact that the foreign *Mitburger* are not true citizens, and, in effect, they are further excluded.[3] It is important to note that the word 'immigrant' is avoided, and the people in question are seen irredeemably as the 'others' among us; the Turks in our midst.

Germany is a nation-state whose identity is becoming ever more problematic as it is threatened by outsiders already inside the 'fortress'. The new asylum law will effectively preclude legal and social admission to many, if not most, of these outsiders. One of the central problems is that the definition of who is a German is

3. Interestingly, *Mitburger* is also used to describe German Jews. Again, this term emphatically marks out as different those people to whom it refers.

based on notions of ethnicity and blood – not civil citizenship.[4] Until *jus sanguinis* makes what to many Germans must appear to be the quantum leap to *jus solis*, the future of foreigners of all types in Germany promises still more insecurity.

References

Bade, Klaus. (ed.) (1987). *Population, Labour and Migration in 19th and 20th Century Germany*, Leamington Spa: Berg.

Brubaker, Rogers. (1992). *Citizenship and Nationhood in France and Germany*, Cambridge MA: Harvard.

Castles, Stephen. (1984). *Here for Good: Western Europe's New Ethnic Minorities*, London: Pluto Press.

Castles, Stephen and Godula Kosack. (1973). *Immigrant Workers and Class Structure in Western Europe*, London: Oxford University Press.

Federal Government Foreign Affairs Division. (1993). *Hostility towards foreigners in Germany: Facts, analyses, arguments.* Publication of the Press and Information Office of the Federal Government Foreign Affairs Division.

Forsythe, D. (1989). German Identity and the Problems of History. In *History and Ethnicity* (eds E. Tonkin, M. McDonald and M. Chapman), ASA Monograph 27, 137–56.

Giddens, Anthony. (1972). *Politics and Society in the Thought of Max Weber*, Basingstoke: Macmillan.

Heidelberger Manifest; 17 June 1981.

Herzfeld, Michael. (1987). *Anthropology Through the Looking Glass: Critical Ethnography in the Margins of Europe*, Cambridge: Cambridge University Press.

Krane, Ronald. (ed.) (1975). *Manpower Mobility across Cultural Boundaries*, Leiden: Brill.

Lewis, Bernard. (1961). *The Emergence of Modern Turkey*, Oxford University Press.

Mandel, R. (1990). Shifting Centres and Emergent Identities: Turkey and Germany in the lives of Turkish *Gastarbeiter*'. In *Muslim*

4. In Germany there appears to be no categorical or conceptual room for a civil definition of citizenship. This is the reason for the complete absence of any immigration policy, despite the fact that close to six million 'foreigners' reside in Germany, many of them having been there for several decades, and many of them having been born there.

Travellers: Pilgrimage, Migration, and the Religious Imagination (eds Dale Eickelman and James Piscatori), London: Routledge and Berkeley University of California Press, 153–71.

Rhoades, R. (1978). Foreign Labour and German Industrial Capitalism 1871–1978: The Evolution of a Migratory System. *American Ethnologist*, **5**, (3), 553–73.

Chapter 6

Nationalism and European Community Integration: The Republic of Ireland

Joseph Ruane

The Maastricht Treaty was the subject of three referenda during 1992. The Danes voted 50.7 per cent against the treaty, the Irish 69.1 per cent in favour, and the French 51 per cent in favour. Most attention has centred on the Danish and French referenda, where the results were close and the survival of the treaty at stake. The Danish rejection was the first blow to a process of accelerated integration which began in the mid-1980s and seemed unstoppable. By September a large NO vote in France was expected; but the close result was disturbing in a country whose support is crucial to the whole process of integration.

In both countries opposition stemmed from concern about the diminution of power to make decisions in the national interest. It pointed to the continued strength of national feeling in the EC, and challenged the assumption that nationalism was in terminal decline. But it also raised the question whether nationalism in the EC should be seen as a legacy of the past, something that will disappear as integration proceeds, or as something more permanent. In fact the view of the EC as a post-nationalist community has always overlooked the extent to which integration is motivated, mediated and underpinned by nationalist concerns.

Nationalism is understood here in a distinctive way, as 'an ideology of the nation', one whose defining characteristic is that it 'places the nation at the centre of its concerns' (Smith 1991: 74). According to this principle the primary concern of each nation is its own well-being. How this is achieved varies with circumstances. It does not necessarily mean a disregard for the well-being of other nations, rule out the possibility of co-operation for the good of all, or insist on absolute sovereignty. Nationalism in this sense is compatible with EC integration; it suffices merely that on balance EC membership advance the well-being of the nation.[1]

I deal with the ways in which nationalism, so defined, is shaping attitudes to EC integration in the Republic of Ireland. The large Irish vote in favour of the Maastricht Treaty has not attracted the same attention as the French or Danish votes, or led commentators to draw lessons for the future. This is in part because its explanation seems clear: Ireland is the largest beneficiary of EC funds per head of population in the EC, and an increase in EC funds was expected to follow the passing of the Treaty. The primacy of economic issues seems confirmed by the issues raised during the campaign. Economic considerations – markets for Irish goods and EC transfers – were most important, followed by concerns about the implications of integration for Irish legislation on abortion and about Irish neutrality. Research since the referendum confirms the importance of these factors in the minds of the voters.[2]

What role did nationalism play in the positions taken on these issues, and how is nationalism mediating and shaping the Irish response to integration? One could play down its role by arguing, for example, that one does not need to be a nationalist to want more money, to dislike armies or to be concerned about abortion or women's rights. But this would detach these issues from current debates about the nature and future of Irish society – debates conducted largely in nationalist terms.

I begin by sketching the goals of Irish nationalism and the extent to which they were realized by the new Irish State. I then look at the different strands of nationalism in the Republic of Ireland today, how they have responded to the intensification of the process of EC integration from the later 1980s, and how they impinge on the integration process. I conclude by drawing out some of the implications for research on EC integration and contemporary nationalism.

1. This concept of nationalism contrasts with those which define it in terms of an insistence on the correspondence of cultural and political boundaries. For example, for Gellner nationalism is 'a political principle that holds that the political and the national unit should be congruent' (Gellner 1983: 1).

2. *Irish Times* 16 December, 1992.